DRIVEN BY HOPE

MEN AND MEANING

JAMES E. DITTES

Westminster John Knox Press
Louisville, Kentucky

Book design by Jennifer K. Cox

Cover design by Kim Wohlenhaus

First edition

Pubished by Westminster John Knox Press
Louisville, Kentucky

This book is printed on acid-free paper that meets the American National Standards Institute Z39.48 standard. ⊗

PRINTED IN THE UNITED STATES OF AMERICA

96 97 98 99 00 01 02 03 04 05 — 10 9 8 7 6 5 4 3 2 1

Library of Congress Cataloging-in-Publication Data

Dittes, James E.
    Driven by hope : men and meaning / James E. Dittes.
      p.   cm.
    ISBN 0-664-25677-5
    1. Men (Christian theology) 2. Hope—Religious aspects—Christianity.
3. Men—Biblical teaching. 4. Masculinity (Psychology) 5. Men—Psychology.
6. Men—Religious life.
    I. Title.
    BT703.5.D55 1996
    261.8'3431—dc20   96-16037

Contents

Preface

This book offers what in these times is an unconventional view: It admires men.

Still more unconventionally, and far from the common view that men are insensitive and shallow, this book supposes that men are inherently religious, afflicted and impelled by a relentless expectancy that life is created to be more whole and holy than we now know. Men wait "with eager longing . . . that the creation itself will be set free from its bondage to decay and will obtain the freedom of the glory of the sons of God."[1] That eager longing is why men sometimes seem to be impatient, coercive, driven, or sometimes disconnected, disgruntled, even self-absorbed. Like all longing, this religious longing is painful; it is also energizing. This book narrates the sorrow and the hope—and the aberrations—that accrue with the soul-felt conviction that life is not (yet) what it is promised to become.

This book finds manhood not in such conventional images of assertion as warrior or king but in the richer expectant postures of priest and pilgrim and, ultimately, in the religiously laden image of expectancy taken by Jesus—that of son.

Re-Deeming Men

Too many writings about men amount to a kind of male bashing. There is something wrong with us, we are told (by both men and women), and we should change. The way we live

1. As Paul wrote to early Christians in Rome (Rom. 8:19–21). "Sons" is more often translated these days as genderless "children," and for good reason. But Paul wrote "sons"; is it possible that he did discern a kind of religious longing and legacy that may be peculiar to men?

our lives is defective, unsatisfactory to our women companions, unsatisfactory to ourselves. Though the specific indictments and recipes vary, the conventional wisdom usually goes something like this:

Men are—and shouldn't be—controlling and dominating, preoccupied with performance and competition, overintellectualizing and underfeeling, defensive and withholding, workaholic, narcissistic, disconnected.

Men should be—and aren't—expressive of feelings, sensitive, vulnerable, caring about relationships, wanting to make commitments—and willing to stop and ask for directions.

As for religion or spirituality, the usual verdict is this: Men lack it and should acquire it.

Sometimes the bashing is limited to this inventory of flawed traits. Sometimes it goes deeper, with a diagnosis of moral or psychological defects ranging from tyrannical power hunger to fragile ego, or maybe simply a poisonous supply of testosterone.

This book goes deeper too, but what it finds in men is value and virtue, not defect and flaw. Even if men do behave the way conventional wisdom says we do, it doesn't mean what conventional wisdom says it means. I want to leave behind the (all-too-easy, all-too-gratifying) diagnosis about what is wrong with men. I want to probe our behavior to expose the nobility it represents. Just maybe the trait usually called "drivenness" should be viewed as commitment; "controlling" may be an honest form of solicitous caring; "withholding" may reflect a realistic, saddened, and profoundly religious caution about giving total and ultimate loyalty to things of this world that don't merit it.

In the political jargon of the day, I propose a fresh spin. Accepting, more or less, the conventional description of men's traits, I want to propose fresh interpretations—interpretations that I find both more authentic and more appreciative. Most books on men's lives want to reform men. This book sets out to *re-deem* men: to deem men's lives, as they are, to be significant, authentic, noble, sensitively and constructively responsive to the deepest ebbs and flows of human destiny.

Masculinity as a Religious Enterprise

In a word, men are deemed here to be *religious*. To be masculine is to be spiritual. The typical man, the typical male behavior, expresses a profoundly and robustly religious attitude.

Whether or not he thinks of himself as religious, whether or not he wants to think of himself as religious, however he spends his Friday evenings or Sunday mornings, the typical man, this book proposes, is religious in the plainest and most elementary sense of that word. To deem a man religious is to claim his serious and earnest engagement with the potentials and the limitations of the human experience. He intuits and trusts that life has a meaning and destiny that lies beyond, elusively but reliably, its presently visible boundaries. He feels called to do his part to enact this meaning and destiny: called, as it were, into a priesthood that mediates and moves life as we know it toward life as it is promised, called into a pilgrimage that searches for blessing and healing beyond the horizon. He is ready, as a priest often is, or a monk or a pilgrim, to renounce close attachments in the world at hand. As he sets his sights beyond his daily life, a man is propelled by the robust religious virtues: faith, hope, love.

Men are inherently religious. *That* is why, this book proposes, we are as we are. It is not because we are victims of a testosterone overdose, or because we are morally defective abusers of others, or because we are afflicted with fragile egos that compel belligerently defensive maneuvers, or because our pathetic narcissism holds us aloof from serious relational commitment. Such diagnoses may be accurate of individual men, or even of all men on occasion, but—like dismissing the prophet or saint for his neuroses—they miss the main point. It is the religious motif that best gives meaning to what can otherwise be characterized as aloofness and withholding, relentless drivenness, impatience, anger, and depression—even the stubborn refusal, when lost, to stop and ask for directions.

In this book's view, when a man drives around and around a strange neighborhood, declining to ask bystanders for directions—which would be to imitate the woman's "relational" mode—what he is doing is trusting a kind of inner light to get him out of his "lostness" and connect him with his destination (his destiny). His is a fundamentally sturdy religious posture, responding with faithfulness to a conviction of revelation and empowerment. It's disloyal to the Holy Spirit, such a man might say, to resort to instruction picked up promiscuously on the street corner. I say more about this in chapter 6 on the magi, the so-called wise men who almost destroyed their mission by abandoning their star and stopping to ask Herod for directions.

Such traits as aloofness or noncommitment or emotional withholding are re-deemed here as expressions of a profoundly accurate religious intuition that life as we know it is a distorted imitation (and promise) of the real thing and cannot command ultimate unreserved devotion. If a man is less enthusiastic than a woman about the daily life they share, it may be because he can see more clearly and sadly beyond its limits. Rather than deem such an attitude depression or defective affect, better re-deem it as the poise of an eschatological waiting for a truer life soon to come. I propose in all seriousness that a man's patient discontent with life as it is mirrors the discontent of God.

In the same way, the traits of zealousness and drivenness and the driving of others, popularly deemed as performance anxiety or hunger for power, may be better re-deemed as accepting a call, however clumsily, to take part in moving life along toward its intended destiny. A man's impatient hunger for life to be renewed mirrors God's hunger. And a man's expectant sense that he is living destined, a sense that breeds both the discontent and the hope that so beleaguer men and their companions, is a God-given gift to be cherished.

This book invites each man to find his ways re-deemed as rightfully a man's ways—and even as God's ways, too.

To be sure, there *is* often abuse and excess—the critics are not inventing such things—so urgent is the discontent and the hunger. This does not challenge the religious spin. Rather, it is the religious motif that gives the best lens for discerning the distortion, the best leverage for correcting it. To regard a man as a priest feeling called to lift life beyond itself, for example, is to remember that men, like any other priests, often commit the idolatry that confuses means and ends. A priest at the altar can forget that his sacraments point beyond themselves and may come to accord them the absolute honor that is deserved only by that to which they point. In the same way, a man may lose sight of the long-range goal—the transforming of life— and come to award (and demand) complete reverence for the means, such as the discipline he imposes on his children or on his own work habits. In chapters 6 through 9, I point out that the magi are tempted to an alliance with the established monarch; that pilgrims are tempted to become shriners or crusaders or colonists; that sons, whose gift is to live in expectancy, are tempted to foreclose that expectancy and usurp fatherhood.

Is there a difference between this holding of men responsible to their religious calling and the conventional scolding of men that I said I would leave behind? I think so. Conventionally, men are *defined* by the abuse and excess—men *are* abusers—but here the distortion is not the defining of men but of a lapse, a side effect of high aspiration. The abuse and excess is just that—not essential to manhood but a fallenness from manhood. It is a sin, if you like. "Sin" implies the contexts of a createdness and of a redeeming that transcend and relativize it. A man is endowed with authentic religious instincts and loyalties, sometimes forsaken by abuse and excess but restorable. In the imagery of later chapters, men may be distorted into playing monarch or shriner or crusader or colonist, but men *are* inherently magi and pilgrims.

Does all this imply a new and monstrous male arrogance, a claim that only men are religious? I hope not. As the early chapters, especially the second, will try to demonstrate, I do think there is something inherent and inevitable about a man's experience that thrusts (and shepherds) him into a religious approach. This is how men come to be religious, I mean to say; women come to be religious by a different path. It can only be a gain for everyone to better recognize these differences.

Men and Women

All too frequently, writing about men takes its agenda from women. Women do have important agendas, and men should take them seriously, but not as a starting point for understanding themselves as men. The starting point for men is men, just as the starting point for women has been women. The best feminist writing seeks to empower and establish feminine identity by probing authentic feminine experience. This book aims to do the same for men. The projects may be parallel, but they need to be independent.

For example, women quite urgently and quite properly raise issues of justice and power between men and women and issues of men's oppression or abuse of women. It has proved easy and conventional to let consciousness-raising about men's injustice to women dominate men's consciousness-raising about their own lives, and men are often urged to be governed by guilt. Though I do not address these issues directly, I hope one result of reading this book will be to enable men to be more responsive to them. No man should let a season pass without hearing and heeding the pain and rage women have to recount. But such hearing and heeding is hardly the best starting place for men's consciousness-raising. Discovering what it is of the sorrow and pain and rage about men's own lives that needs voicing and heeding is probably the best preparation for listening to women. The oppression we inflict is bound to the oppression we endure.

In tandem with these issues in the public forum, the agenda is sometimes set for men by women's more personal frustrations with us. When women find enigma or dissatisfaction in men's behavior, it is easy to take for granted that it is men's responsibility to accommodate. In my view, men need to be aware of such frustration if we are going to negotiate successful relationships, but we do not need to be governed by it. To recognize another's need is not the same as letting that need become a demand. Men should not adopt women's interpretations and diagnoses of our traits—women's definition of men; rather, we should be prompted to discover our own interpretations, our own self-definition. That is the project of this book. We men need to know who we are; only then can we deal meaningfully with what women think we are and with their needs and expectations.

Sometimes women are allowed or invited to set the agenda in another way. Some men (and some women) find it easy to suppose (and they may be right) that men would be better human beings if we were more like women. Because *social* wholeness requires the balance, blending, and equality between men and women that it does, it has been easy to surmise that *individual* wholeness requires a similar internal balance between male and female traits. (Sometimes anyone who resists such androgyny as a therapeutic formula is accused of resisting social justice.) This usually translates to making men more "vulnerable," more "sensitive," more "expressive," more "relational," or to "getting in touch with the feminine within." That may be a good goal, but is not a good starting point. Rather than such androgynous gender-blending, this book proposes that there are plenty of neglected *masculine* traits or personas— magi, pilgrim, son—that deserve getting in touch with and giving significance to.

This book is not concerned (though I am) with other matters that one might expect to encounter in a book on gender and religion, such as with men's or women's roles in churches or with the strategies and etiquette of things like inclusive language in worship and gender balance of religious imagery.

I do need to acknowledge, however, one apparent alliance with (and even reliance on) an item of the feminist agenda. Women have called our attention to something we need to notice too, though our purposes are quite different. They have pointed out that the expressions of religiosity most abundant in scripture, in theological thought, in liturgical customs, and in religious institutional structures are predominantly male in character. How could it be otherwise, given our culture's male-dominated history? This makes these patterns often inadequate for women in expressing their own religiosity. Women have testified eloquently to the misfit and have set out to remedy the deficit of feminine-relevant imagery and expression by fashioning appropriate new imagery. That is an urgent project with which I have not the slightest quarrel. In its own way this book is a parallel effort.

Indeed, the gender bias that makes traditional religious imagery not useful to women should make it particularly useful to men. If biblical accounts and traditional theological formulations are largely expressions of male religiosity, a book like this should explore these areas as disclosing that distinctively male religiosity. This book occasionally ventures to do just that, and to do so may seem a rampant purloining and exclusiveness. But I do not believe this is male territorial aggressiveness; rather, I see it as merely acknowledging and legitimately using for our purposes the biases that women experience and, from their point of view, legitimately protest.

But in accepting—even welcoming and exploiting—the feminist critique that the Bible and theology are male-biased, I offer one huge caveat: The male experience that I find portrayed in the Bible is by no means limited to the male experience discerned by the feminists. The patriarchs, like men of our time, are not just patriarchal; they are also homeless exiles and pilgrims possessed of profound faith and hope. Who is yanked into more unsettled and tormented lives than figures like Adam, Noah, Abraham, Isaac, Esau, Jacob, Joseph, Moses, Jesus, Paul? Who better knows forsakenness than these archetypal

men of sorrows? Not just victimizers, biblical men are host-
ages, too, to promises dangled and broken. Where can we find
men more entangled in the shadows of their own destiny, more
faithful about discerning destiny in the shadows? The Bible is
rich in testimonies of male experience.

Intimately Theological

Much religious writing about men takes its agenda from
nonreligious resources. It is important to explore the resources
of psychology, biology, and anthropology, to integrate our find-
ings with theological reflection, and to make the results available for the professional use of the clergy. But that is not what
this book ventures. This is not the book for you if you want a
summary of the literature in the psychology of masculinity and
an adapting of this psychology, with or without a theological
veneer, for use in a religious or parish context.

This may be a book for you if you want to think about *religious* dimensions. It ventures an unabashedly theological re-
visioning of men's lives. It regards men first and foremost as religious beings (whether or not men regard themselves in this
way). It sees men as adopting religious strategies for dealing
with religious dilemmas and rhythms. These religious dimensions of a man's experience are taken here as primary. Understanding a man religiously, theologically, may help to understand him psychologically, not the other way around.

As for a minister's concern with the pastoral care of men,
this book is not a handbook but it may be a model. It illustrates
how I would approach a pastoral or a counseling relation with
another man.

Because it is theological, it is intimate. Theology should
voice the throbs of the human soul—though this voice is too
often hijacked by those who prefer abstraction and remoteness, as though phobic to the throbs. The book aspires to be
personal and conversational, as conversational as the printed
page allows. I invite you to regard what follows as my way of
saying *This is how it is with me. Is it this way with you. . . . or
a little different . . . . . or very different?* Where do you say, *How
did you know me?* and where do you say, *You don't know me?*
The book will have been most successful if it frequently lies

face down, unfinished, while you ponder your own experience. (And I thank Roger Johnson for the compliment of treating an earlier book of mine just that way.) The response of turning my book face down, unfinished, while you ponder will be our own way of finding replenished life in incompleteness, in expectancy.

Part I

THE SHADOWS OF DESTINY

Is That All There Is?

1

Men are expectant. Men live a life that feels chronically destined, ever on the verge—intended for something that is never quite arrived at, an unending not-yet, the perpetual pilgrimage of almost, a prolonged tumescence. Something beckons and promises a man but also eludes and teases—something hinted at in the life he knows but something unmistakably beyond, just beyond naming, ever beyond grasping, intimate and sure and yet elusive—that life which is truly his and yet never his. A man treasures his life as a gift, mourns it as a gift never unwrapped. All men know that at home, at work, in our private dreams for ourselves, there is a fruition waiting, a destination, a destiny. And all men know ourselves excruciatingly separated from that promise, surely destined but just as surely unarrived. A man looks back at the end of an hour or a day, at the end of a career or a marriage, and finds promises stunted and shunted. Is that all there is? He knows it isn't; he knows it is. Chronically destined. A man looks ahead beyond the horizon of visible reality to the reality of the almost visible, and he burgeons with hope. Chronically destined. A man learns to live with constancy in the in-between. A man learns how to live in the shadow of his own destiny.

In everyday terms, it's just-as-soon-as. Just as soon as I clear my desk or my calendar or my debts. Just as soon as I clear things up with my boss or my wife. Just as soon as the kids are older. Just as soon as there is more money in the bank. Just as soon as my boss retires. Just as soon as we get out of this neighborhood. Just as soon as I finish this training. Just as soon as I tell my father off. Just as soon as I quit smoking. Just as soon as I have time to exercise. Mundane expression of apocalyptic hope, just-as-soon-as is how we build serviceable bridges across the ravines of hopelessness.

In a longer-term view, it's pausing when allowed—as in the conventional "midlife crisis"—to ponder goals and their elusiveness, to look back with the serious question *Is that all there is?* and with the more searing *If only . . .*, and to look forward with a renewed but familiar blend of expectancy and resignation—sometimes impetuously determined to seize the hope, sometimes succumbing to the resignation.

It's like any other mature romantic longing: satisfaction eluding even as it is attained, love replenishing longing even as it quenches it.

In religious terms, men are afflicted with hope. Hope means living a life that awaits, longingly, a fulfillment that must come from beyond the everyday domain, since it doesn't seem to come within that domain. Life is lived—and is meant to be lived—in a kind of in-betweenness. Life is not (yet) what it is meant to be; life is meant to be what it is not (yet). A man lives in the kingdom of God but also knows himself separated from that kingdom. Life is in between, on the way, not comfortably here, not yet there, destined.

Men make promises and know keenly the anguish of finding them unkept. We are reminded relentlessly of our failures to others. But men also believe promises and know the keener anguish of finding *them* unkept, notably the promise that we can live our own life fully and freely. It is a powerful engine, the sorrow of living with that promise unmet.

The Bible tells it clearly, from the beginning: paradise wanting. Adam looked around Eden and asked, *Is that all there is?* The sorrow of incompleteness is man's from the outset—part of creation, not a symptom of sin or fall—just as the sorrow of a blameless life cut short on a cross reveals redemption, not sin. This sorrow of incompleteness, life chronically destined, is what is offered to man as the avenue to wholeness and holiness. Life in want; life detoured, in a closet, a gift not yet unwrapped—this must be the most relentless theme of the Bible, recounted in its many rich variations: faithful affirmation of what lies in store, an affirmation so vivid it measures excruciatingly the deficit at hand. The Bible shouts (and whispers) the triumphant story of men's wanting: Life is abundant and authentic, but not yet.

The patriarchs lived by the savor of promises to come true for generations to follow. Patriarchs have a bad name in our day, portrayed as arbitrary wielders of misogynous power. But the Bible makes clear what it means to be a patriarch. It means, with Noah, to leave home behind, to leave land behind, to be set adrift (Gen. 7). It means, with Abram, to live alien in his own land ("By faith he stayed for a time in the land he had been promised, as in a foreign land"—Heb. 11:9a) and to break camp at the age of seventy-five and set out on a pilgrimage he knew not where (Gen. 12). It means, with Jacob, to long for a birthright not his yet somehow due him; to labor long for the dreamed-of bride, only to have to do it all again; to wrestle with an angel for a blessing, only to win a wound (Gen. 25, 27, 29, 32). It means, with Esau, to plead, *Haven't you saved a blessing for me?* (Gen. 27). It means, with Moses, to commit forty years to a wandering pilgrimage, heading vaguely for a promised land eventually glimpsed in the haze across the river (just as he was once permitted to view deity only from the back side, Ex. 33:23) but never gained more closely than that view from Mount Pisgah (Deut. 3, 32, 34). (We may know Mount Pisgah better from the Rev. Martin Luther King Jr.'s remark, on the last day of *his* life, about having "been to the mountain"; or perhaps we know it from our own wistful visit to that terrain, as we see life unfolding ahead, without us.) It means, with the prophets (Isaiah, Jeremiah, Amos, Hosea), while living in exile and apostasy, to commit selves, body and soul, to telling a message, like Sisyphus, that never gets heeded. It means, with Job, to pursue relentlessly the urgent questions that echo in the canyons of his very manly grief unanswered. It means, with Jonah, to confront his mission impossible, choose not to accept it, and thus live out his life in the dwindling shadow of a withered bush.

The New Testament images are of a still starker kind. From the beginning (Matt. 1, 2), Joseph the father who was not the father; the would-be wise men who strayed off course and unwittingly instigated Herod's slaughter of innocent children; on to Jesus' elusive preaching about a kingdom that is among us but isn't, his commitment to divine mission that rendered him homeless and forsaken, his paradoxical claiming of life in death; and on again to Paul's conviction of living on the verge of a redemption almost-here-but-not-quite-yet, an in-betweenness and wary expectancy that Christian theology invites us to persist in. Paul's affirmation (Rom. 8) that nothing can separate us from the love of God reminds us that everything threatens to do so. Finally, the good news ends with the extravagantly apocalyptic Revelation of all earthly domain destroyed for its salvation.

As the Bible reminds us with vivid authority, we live in an excruciating blend of hope and despair; we live in want, in the shadow of the birthright we don't have, born to broken promises. And it reminds us, with equally vivid authority, that we indeed *live* in that shadow.

Augustine, church father that he was (early bishop and theologian, 354–430), may have provided us with the first and best pithy characterization of living in the shadow of one's own destiny. He set out, a millennium and a half ago, to recount in midlife what it was like to grow up a man, the first effort ever at a spiritually revealing autobiography; he called it *Confessions*. He sounded the keynote—his version of *Is that all there is?*—in the opening paragraph: "Our hearts are restless until they find their rest in [God.]" That's a marvelously two-faced sentence, which reflects in its ambiguity a blend of trust and despair any man can recognize. Does it affirm that there is ultimate surcease and satisfaction? Yes, emphatically. Does it also imply that the heart's rest is so ultimate, so removed, as to leave lots of room for the restlessness to thrive? Yes, that too. Only God can calm and keep us, but our relation to God is elusive and problematic. So our hearts are restless. Setting our religious sights much lower than Augustine's, *we* might say, our hearts are restless until we find the right partner—or the right job, or the right car—and we would be at once affirming the expectant hope and confessing the persisting hunger, in our own way affirming with Augustine both the destiny and its shadows.

A man sorrows because he knows himself in both senses of "know," and they don't match. There is the subjective intuitive familiarity: the way one "knows" another person, can pick out the shape of the back of his head in a crowd, can read between the lines of what he is saying to know what he means. A man intuitively knows himself and his destiny with this kind of intimacy and richness—the way Adam "knew" Eve for example, the way all the biblical patriarchs "knew" their women, perhaps the way all lovers know each other, idealized. Then there is the more objective, unidealized, deconstructed, cold-light-of-day, matter-of-fact rational knowing, the way a scientist knows a fact, as a datum, tests it. When a man checks out the hard facts of his life as he knows them, they don't match (yet?) the rich person he knows himself to be.

Jesus is seen as Savior just because he knows intimately both human destiny and its shadows. It is precisely because he is recognized as a "man of sorrows" (Isa. 53:3; "suffering" in NRSV) that Jesus is recognized as one who both partakes profoundly in the human experience and also leads the way beyond it.

We know ourselves as men of sorrows.

Sorrow is like grief but more lasting. A man doesn't outlive sorrow the way he can outlive grief. He must simply live out the sorrow. Grief looks backward and can be outlived by looking forward. Grief is the soul wrenched by loss of what once was. It can gradually be let go. Grief abates; sorrow persists. Sorrow looks ahead and mourns what appears missing as far as one can see, the divergence between life visible and life intended. Sorrow is the soul teased. *Is that all there is?*

Re-Deeming Men as Men of Sorrows

The Impatience of Hope

Living chronically destined endows a man with a penchant, often misplaced, for wresting his destiny, for subduing the tease and claiming the prize. So men—as we are abundantly reminded and often scolded—are driven to achieve, to perform, to manage, to overpower, to control, to compete, to conquer, self-coerced to accomplish their own birthright, flinging themselves across the persistent tantalizing gap from the actual to the intended, from the daily reality to the promised reality beyond—as though Moses could leap from Mount Pisgah across the Jordan. A man's trust that he is destined often lures him to chase mirages of destiny. So he dreams of conquest—sexual, financial, athletic, or workplace—in verbal dueling, in petty tyrannies.

Or, if the spiritual impatience does not become a fight to

claim destiny, then flight. Flight—into drink or drugs or drums or some other lunge across the boundaries of settled life to pursue a mirage of "liberation"—passes, for the moment, as emancipation from the strictures and structures that seem to deny a man his destiny.

This impatient goal-drivenness *is* masculinity in most conventional discussion, usually deplored as destructive and distorting, as of course it often is. Conventional wisdom likes to pronounce this trait as a gender-based moral flaw or to diagnose it as medical ("testosterone") or psychiatric ("fragile ego"). Here we understand it as derived from the male plight of living chronically destined, religious in energy though seldom in effect. For the religious lust for destiny is so urgent that it gets invested in counterfeits of destiny—as religious faith often does. Close up, the mirages do fade, as conventional wisdom is quick to flog men for; they *are* futile, self-defeating, and damaging to others. The man in conquest or flight remains unarrived, still destined. His lust for destiny is too deep to be satisfied by such glib counterfeits, too archetypal, too rooted in the very core of his manhood. This is a hunger of the soul, a hunger of the soul for itself. Deepest in the belly is not fire but ache.

This scurrying for a lightening of the shadows and a brightening of the destiny deserves to be recognized for the profoundly religious impulse it expresses. *Is that all there is?* Faith resounds no! More *is* destined, for a man and for those he loves. A man feels his energies conscripted by that faith. Don't scold him for answering that call, though grieve with him when he discovers he is pursuing a counterfeit. Honor his faith and commitment and help him to enlarge it: Let him expand his trust from the destiny to the shadows, too, until they are seen as avenues to the destiny, not just barriers. A man living more comfortably in the sorrow of his shadowed destiny has less need to lunge blindly for the mirages of destiny.

The Patience of Hope

Impatient pursuit or impatient flight is not the only response of religious imperative to the plight of living destined. Men also respond with sorrow and patience, sometimes excessive. They wait. Their faith vouches that life at hand is not (yet) whole enough to merit wholehearted investment. So they wait. Conventional wisdom—verging on caricature—rebukes this response as aloofness, alienation, withholding. Such traits are redeemed here as expressions of religious awe and humility, expressions of hope and its sorrows. It is profoundly painful to live life as a gift never unwrapped, to exercise phantom limbs. It is an anguish kept hidden. Who dares acknowledge a destiny unreached, a selfhood aborted? Who dares acknowledge a destiny? Here we dare admit such things, dare even to honor the confident patience with which men endure and thrive while living between the promise and the frustration of their own destiny.

The Hunger of Hope

A man experiences life as given to him incomplete. His birthright endowment is a primordial deficit, a deficit that is part of his nature, a deficit that defies remedy, a lostness that defies saving, as though a man is allotted a degree of emptiness to be born with, lived with, and died with. Or is it the same thing to say that a man is endowed with a dream, a vision beyond the here and now, an unquenchable conviction that there is more to come. A man is endowed with an unquenchable hunger. A man is endowed with an unquenchable hope. The hope *is* the hunger. Hunger is *for* something, something not at hand but promised. The hunger of *Is that all there is?* breeds the faith *There must be more.* The conviction *There must be more* breeds the discontent of *Is that all there is?*

A man knows himself as "wanting"—in both dreadful senses of that word. He feels *in want*, defective, in deficit, missing something. And he *wants*, yearns for that extra something he feels sure is intended for him. He also knows the delicious sense of wanting, craving, afflicted both with the sublime faith that there is something more in store for him and with the underside of that faith, the sublime despair that he is separated from that promise.

What does a man want? Sigmund Freud never directed to men that famous vexed and impatient question, "What do women want?" He seems to have thought, like most of us, that a real man *doesn't* "want" or that a real man, if he does find himself in want, doesn't yield to it, but renounces and conquers any "wanting." But he was wrong. So we all are when we bravely pretend otherwise, that we don't want for anything and that to be in want doesn't hurt painfully. Men do live in want, and what

we want is not so mysterious or so unseemly. A man, like anyone else, wants to live his *own* life and to live it *fully:* life authentic and abundant. Every man's chronic sorrow is for his
unlived life. Conquering that sorrow comes to claim every
man's prime energies. But it will not be quelled, and the strat-
agems to defy it or deny it only lead to further distortions, the
more notable distortions, the ones that most invite rebuke and
regret.

Living destined, living in want, is not like living amputated.
Something is missing, but not something once held and now dis-
appeared. This is not a deficit measured by the past; that is called
aging and is a loss that can be coped with. That is grief; this is
sorrow. This is deficit measured by promise, intent, destiny,
missing birthright, exile from Eden, wilderness wandering in
quest of promised land. What is missing is what I *know* is there
for me; it's just *not* there for me: the zest of greeting the morning, the sexual abandon of the night, the tender steady affection
of family, a confident feeling—"Yes!"—when I pull into the parking lot at work or when I walk into a roomful of people, the glow
of having made a lasting impact on something. "Burnout" is the
way we usually account for our zestlessness. But that is inexact;
it implies a former blazing trajectory, a payload delivered, abundant light once shed. Our actual feeling is more like that of a fuse
sputtering, a light flickering, a blast still to come.

So a man feels his life derived, secondary, removed, adjunct, truncated, conscripted, indentured, sidelined, a token, an
IOU, a stand-in, a promise for the real thing—not the real thing
but a definite promise. A full-dress rehearsal. The athlete—
trained, disciplined, and warmed up—still waiting for the starting whistle. The basketball rolling around the rim. Watching a
movie or reading a book that has been highly praised and wondering why. In a closet, poised and aching to burst out "any
time now" into that other world that is promised and promising, the one you belong in, the one perpetually just out of reach.
This is fundamental to manhood.

Pangs of the Hunger

It's as though we were haunted by the fact that the fount of
life belongs to the other gender, that our loins and breasts are
empty, fated by anatomy to remain adjunct to life.

It's as though we were haunted by the disquiet, never resolved, never even recognized, still lingering from what was truly our first romance, our first broken heart, when the boy longs for a totally unreserved bond with the woman who means life to him, his mother, but longs futilely because she has other agendas and because she belongs to another man.

It's as though we were haunted by that boyhood longing for companionship with our father, a longing inevitably sabotaged by the fact that it is polluted with our own sense of rivalry with that same father, with all the turbulent and troubling emotions of anger and fear that rivalry breeds.

It's as though we were relentlessly cheered on by culture to emulate titanic heroes of great prowess and glamour, but heroes conjured out of fantasy and never reachable.

It's as though the young black men consigned by a faithless society to nurse their bruised hoop dreams on shabby street corners are but the least disguised and most unfair form of the way the social system discards all men whose ambitions it has recruited.

It's as though we were cast by women's coaching and promise into roles and scripts we enact assiduously, only and always to discover that the rewards we thought we contracted for never came.

It's as though we were haunted by the devastating psychological separation forced on a boy but not on a girl. Girls may and must identify with their mothers. But to rescue and mold his identity as male, a boy has to put distance between himself and the one who gave him life, his mother. A man has had to choose between maleness and intimacy with life.

It's as though early on, because we were boys, we were taught one mantra with which to address all ills: "just as soon as I get bigger"—an incessant conjuring we sounded for our first ten years (until we enlarged our repertory of "just-as-soon-as" mirages). We found it immensely reassuring to suppose that the deficit, all the "can't do" and "if only" of our life, was that easily named and that surely remedied. Whatever was wrong at home, at school, in the playground, in solitude, whatever bafflement, whatever impotence: Just wait until I'm bigger. So we learned to muster bigness as the panacea for all ills, and we still do; we rely on bigness as the one relentless solution: a big biceps, bank account, vocabulary, desk, car, score, and, of course, a huge erection. But our bigness is never big enough. So we extend that mantra of the first ten years —"just as soon as I get bigger"—through all the decades. But the bigness imagined or achieved doesn't work; it is never a match for the hollowness. The "can't do" and the "if only" prevail, unbudging, just as much a part of a man as the whiskers he tries to lop off daily.

It's as though we were haunted by the dismaying fact that that which most defines our manhood, our erect penis, is a sometime thing, mostly absent, sometimes even when most wanted, but also intrusively insistent, conniving us into embarrassment or peril or disloyalty. This manhood of ours is separated from us, a phallic mystery with a mind of its own.

It's as though our grandest sexual climax renders us limp and unready, the moment of supreme potency also enforcing more than a moment of impotence.

It's as though the principal modeling our fathers provide for us is a long-sustained lesson in how to be absent, how to impact through remote control. It's as though manhood were thus defined by its remove from the source and throb of life.

Of course we hate wearing a condom. It reminds us too vividly of how we experience everything, sheathed and insulated.

Of course sometimes the containment overwhelms and longing denied erupts as longing distorted; we take reckless risks, in a desperate lunge to transplant ourselves instantly into full experience. Of course we plow heedlessly and disastrously from the breakdown lane into traffic.

Of course we have midlife crises. It's one time that culture permits, more or less, the sorrow to surface, to experience the throbbing discontent that our life is missing the point and the promise, the urgent hunger/fear/hope that there must be more. *Is that all there is?* Of course not, it never was; but it may not be until midlife that we are allowed, maybe, to ask. And yearning so long contained may erupt rashly.

Of course we make fools of ourselves trying so desperately to make full men of ourselves, trying to unwrap the gift of life, to get off the sidelines and into the action—call it macho if you need to—trying to snatch and engineer and invent the birthright never known.

Of course we convert shame into swagger and lies (most often to ourselves) about the size of our bank account, our penis, our address book, our biceps, our retirement bonus, our obituary, or the crowd that will assemble at our funeral. Culture teaches us to scramble and to claim an upsized "more" just when we most grieve. *Is that all there is?*

Ritualizing the Shadows

The culture provides ways, safely contained, to name and claim the sorrow out loud. Ritualized moments like the midlife crisis give men authorization and vocabulary to acknowledge the wanting. The same rituals that define manhood define the sorrow: *Something's missing. Is that all there is? Haven't you saved a blessing for me?*

New fathers have long been expected to pace out their nervous irrelevance and helplessness, though many now struggle to disguise it with such labors as coaching breathing. Older fathers sometimes are still allowed to "give away" their daughters as brides with a blustery self-consciousness that fails to hide the grief that the time with her has come to an end without reaching completion. Gay men are offered the notion of closet to account for their experience of being separated from their own life. The athletic prowess that men so expertly and bravely practice vicariously before the television is transparent transportation into a rich other world that men struggle to inhabit more intimately than their daily world, with no less faith and no less illusion than any other religious enterprise.

So too with the other worlds men create and inhabit in barroom and locker room bluster, or just as often in private musings or in annual broadside Christmas letters or letters written for class reunions. Here it is permitted to inhabit boldly the secret paradises and promised lands in which bosses and in-laws are told off and other justice heroically achieved, in which all problems at work are transcended, in which relationships with women are satisfying and unproblematic, in which children are responsive and productive, in which life is one and won. All are assurances that articulate, in their own ways, the persistent wanting so routinely unarticulated.

Then there is the idealization committed at the retirement dinner or the fiftieth anniversary party or the eightieth birthday, in which a man's life is portrayed in words that give perverse expression to the wanting that has for so long been inarticulate and unallowed. Destiny is named and claimed, un-shadowed, just as though it has all come true, vaunting a pil-grimage completed that was perhaps scarcely begun.

All the endings without completion—the end of a marriage, a vacation, a business meeting, a business lunch, a sexual ad-venture, a weekend visit with grandchildren or parents—kindle the gnawing, primordial, too-familiar feeling: *"Is that all there is?"* Panic-stricken, we scarcely dare whisper to ourselves (but we do), "Will it be that way when I die?"

These ways that the sorrow is named out loud among us of-ten have the overtones of religious rituals. For this is a wanting of cosmic proportions, one that can't be understood apart from the rhythms of religious quest, the pangs of a soul hunger that seems to be there from birth, triggered by a vision of promises from beyond.

Yet the sorrow of living chronically destined in hope is more archetypal and primordial than can be readily embraced by these homemade rituals. Our sorrow is contained too in story and myth. Legendary heroes such as Odysseus and Ae-neas, Abraham and Moses—and Oedipus, too, made by Sig-mund Freud so emblematic of maleness—are wanderers and pilgrims in search of a promised land they intuit as their des-tiny, pursuing the arrival that will make good the deficits of their lives heretofore.

We retell the stories in chapter 3 of two figures that stand in our consciousness as emblems of manhood: Adam and Oedi-pus. Their stories echo in our own lives—but not, we need to discover, in the way we are usually taught. It is for their hor-rendous misdeeds that conventional wisdom makes Adam and Oedipus into Everyman. Each is supposed to have committed sin in a fashion so huge and primordial, so "original," that the deed crashes through history and defines every man's male-ness. But that conventional wisdom is a misreading (or at least a selective reading) bordering on the slanderous. The actual stories tell something different; they tell of spiritual hunger and a courageous quest to redeem the promise of a dignified des-tiny. It is time to let Adam and Oedipus and ourselves out of the closet as men of spiritual yearning, courage, and integrity.

First, however, it is time to go back to our beginnings, to trace our own histories, to discover how we, like Adam, were created as the men we are.

Endowed as Men

2

Living in want is not an injury to be fixed, an accident to be recovered from, an ill-fitting garment to be shed. It is not acquired, not optional, not the product of an individual life history. It is decidedly not a flaw to be atoned for. Living in want is constituent of what it means to be a man, a product of a man's spiritual genes. Men are supposed to live in want, in deep spiritual hunger, in the shadows of their own destiny, desperately hopeful. It is a part of manhood to be welcomed, embraced, lived by, not against. A man is more of a man, not less, for living in want. Sorrow and shadows belong to the order of creation, not to the Fall. And they belong, too, to the process of redeeming, where we encounter the paradoxical power of finding one's life by losing it, the power that sorrow and shadows deliver.

If this proposal has truth, we should be able to track what it is about becoming a man that destines him to live destined, in that blend of sorrow and hope recounted in the preceding chapter, discontent and restless with life as he knows it, aspiring to the life he knows is intended for him even as he is alienated from it.

This chapter ventures to do that tracking; quite explicitly, to trace how it is that the very same formative processes that make a man a man also make him "in want." It aims to make developmentally plausible the central theme that there is a distinctively male brand of discontent that is inevitable, even natural: To be a man *is* to be in want, achingly restless, primed

15

for pilgrimage, chronically destined, ever unarrived. To be a man is to discover, in ways given only to men, the promise and plight of the human predicament. To be a man is to be privileged to a keen sense of the spiritual wisdom that life is found in its losing.

This proposal pushes uphill against the longtime presumption that what defines the real man is exactly the opposite of sorrow or confession of want: that a real man defies, conquers, overlooks, rises above discomforts and disappointments and deficits and whatever happenstance may occasion them; that a real man erases the shadows and seizes his destiny. Seeming disappointments are due to events that can be confronted and subdued, man vs. trauma and tragedy; that's the conventional wisdom. Here we propose that real men are men of sorrows, that the reality of manhood is in the shadows of man's destiny.

Anatomy as Destiny

To track what may be distinctive and intrinsic to maleness, we obviously need to turn first, at length and very explicitly, to anatomy—especially to our very first, quite unglamorized, raw encounters with our own genitals.

Here we run immediately into a skeptical challenge from conventional wisdom: "It's *men* who feel themselves born into deficit?" Conventional wisdom—which in this case generally means Freudian wisdom—has long assured us that it is women who feel themselves anatomically deprived; "penis envy," it is called. "Something's missing" has been supposed to be the female cry. It is women who have been anatomically endowed with a sense of emptiness that requires fulfilling. Boys have the prized organ, girls do not, so it must be girls who live in want.

Furthermore, quite apart from Freudian orthodoxy, commonsense wisdom would have it that the themes discussed in these chapters are human themes, not reserved to men. All people, *as* people, regardless of gender, see their lives as amiss, askew, falling far short of what they have heard promised to them and what they have promised. Is it some new mutation of male arrogance to claim exclusive possession of disappointment?

The conventional wisdom is right and wise and important, as far as it goes. But it is our purpose here to try to lift up and clarify what special accent or spin is put on the experience of wanting by the fundamental experience of maleness. The challenge is to focus, not to exclude. How do *men* "want" and how do *men* come to be "in want"? To pose such a question is not to deny that it could be equally important and fruitful to ask the same question about women. It is to probe for the special insights that come into focus by narrowing the lens. By talking about men we can say things that describe and explain the mood of "wanting," insights we would never reach if we were not to ask about men in particular.

As for the conventional Freudian wisdom, based on pride and envy about having and not having a penis, it is important to recognize that this is about boys and girls, prepuberty boys and girls. We should picture kids furtively exploring their bodies, giggling and teasing, exchanging crude jokes in tight all-boy or all-girl huddles on the playground. As young boys and girls we *are* exaggeratedly attentive, as Freud says, to such things as penises and their absence, just as, when puberty strikes, we will become fascinated with breasts and their absence. Prepuberty *is* a setup for boys to feel, or claim, they have it all and for girls to sense that something is missing. And we never entirely outgrow such boyhood and girlhood.

However, even on Freud's terms, there is more than pride for boys in this period. Pride sets up for danger, and there is risk and threat in boyhood, ominous foreboding that things, especially things male, are not securely as grand as they seem. The very prizing of the penis, like any other idol-making, leaves boys feeling vulnerable. There are fears over its inadequacy, as differences in size and appearance burden appreciation of the prize with questions about normalcy and flaws. These fears loom huge as every boy feels left behind by the blustering tales of sexual exploit abounding on the playground and in film. There are fears of loss, fantasies of castration that can't be shaken; the penis seems so exposed, and hostility nearby is readily suspected. So here may be one crucial model, one prototype for male wanting: "I have it, but maybe not securely," or "I have it, but it may not be as big as it should be," or "I have it but it's not big enough to qualify me as one of 'them,' those real men that are represented by father, brothers, and the tough guys at school, or on TV, or in the magazines."

While there is, to be sure, a lot of such prepuberty

childhood left in each of us, there is also much more. When puberty strikes, a boy's attention shifts from penis to erect penis, phallus, and to ejaculation. Here are intriguing mysteries of a compellingly new kind. If anything can make a person feel a moment of communion with life itself, bonded with the holy—whatever the extravagant phrase, it's not too extravagant for the experience—it must be every boy's first amazed experiences of grasping that throbbing, taut, excruciatingly tingling erection and of being bathed in those startling spurts of warm semen, surging unbidden from the depths of who knows where. The encounter is so unique, so intense, so riveting, it raises huge quandaries, quite beyond the capacity of any boy or man to cope with. These are quandaries of persistent religious perplexity, quandaries such as: If something is that intense, that pleasurable, that exalting, that surprising, it must be supremely good or bad, but which? Is it gift or curse; is it to be welcomed and encouraged or shunned, shouted and shared or held secret, enjoyed or feared? But perhaps most of all, certainly most relevant here, it raises the excruciating question about the locus, the source of these startling new entities, phallus and orgasm, these new promising scary secrets of life. Are they part of me or somehow a stranger?

The inevitable and imprinting dilemma each man experiences is that, while erection and ejaculation are the very essence and emblem of his manhood, this manhood is utterly capricious and fugitive, quite beyond control or even understanding. It rises and comes unbidden, even when unwanted. It often appears most fiercely in the stupor of the night. The boy wakes to his manhood or to startling evidence that it has come and gone, now but an eerie memory, delicious enough to be intimately his and shadowy enough to seem a strange visitor.

Daytime, too, the erection comes as a strange visitor, unannounced and unexplained and certainly shamefully unwanted: The family doesn't understand, but they probably do, why you won't leave the supper table with the others. Everyone in class knows why you carry the notebook with you, desperate shield slung low, to the blackboard. And you become awkwardly mute on the beach, belly down on the blanket. This treasured and intimate emblem of your manhood is an alien visitor from outer space.

That alien visitor can be tyrannically demanding. You don't

want to sneak off and masturbate, or pick up a partner who is not really a partner, or forcefully insist against a partner's unmistakable unwillingness. You really don't, but *it* insists. So you obey, but you feel captured, somehow in thrall to something—as central and basic as it is at the core of your own identity—that is not you and calls you away from yourself.

You feel there must be a devastating difference between your sexuality and a woman's. Her sexuality seems self-contained—she's the one who can say yes or no; she doesn't really need a man—while yours is out there demanding a partner. A partner: one more aspect of your sexuality that you can't control, that leaves you repeatedly wanting.

But soon enough the capriciousness and the otherness works in reverse. The time comes that just when the erection is most wanted it balks, stubbornly absent when most commanded. *Because* commanded, we come to recognize. This manhood so intimate and so basic is, like a father, not there after all for the wish or the command but must be more gently wooed. But that's not "manly." Chancy wooing, when you are unsure about how to do it and have no guarantees about results—that seems appropriate for those mysterious and essentially alien creatures called girls, but how can your own manhood be like that?

Or its visit is annoyingly and embarrassingly brief, foreshortened and grieved. It's there one minute in glorious promise. Then, suddenly and quite contrary to your own intentions, and contrary to the promise it makes on your behalf to your partner, it's all over, come and gone, turned phantom. With carefully contained chagrin, you must offer substitutes or wait, limply. This must be one of the crucially devastating ways a man is primed to feel all the forms of "wanting." Going through the motions, closeted, hitting the wall, a token, cheated, on the verge, hostage: All these words fit this experience. This must be one of the key lessons, but only one, that to be a man is to wonder *Is that all there is?* and to grieve *Something's missing.*

Erection, then, is given as emblem of life and of manhood, key to male identity—but, in the deed not given, withheld, or imposed capriciously, leaving a legacy of wanting.

And not just phallus but so, too, with the other identifying emblem of maleness, ejaculation. It comes when it wants to, not when you want: often sooner; sometimes later than you would choose; sometimes by total surprise, insistent in the night, out of nowhere; sometimes stubbornly resistant, orgasm excruciatingly "on the verge," this life force from your very bowels which is, on occasion, so determinedly not yours.

But conventional, or perhaps feminist, wisdom rejoins: Aren't girls—far more dramatically and obviously than these male subtleties—estranged by their very femaleness, by their menstrual flow, by "the curse"?

Of course girls cope with a massive intrusion, a decidedly unbidden and unannounced alien invader. No man has a right to minimize that; we are not engaging in a competition of suffering. But one difference is crucial to notice, to define the male's experience as clearly as possible.

The initiation experiences that the body insists on at puberty for boys (first ejaculation) and for girls (first menstruation) are both loaded with ambivalence, the ambivalence that is awe, an excruciating mixture of wonder and wariness. But the balance between blessing and curse is skewed differently. For girls it is the wonder that persists and finally survives, for boys the wariness. In the short run, the girl tends to feel afflicted by menstruation, an unwelcome, undeserved intrusion. But in the long run it is promise, bond to wonder, the wonder of giving new life. For boys, the time scale is reversed: The wonder and glory are immediate but ephemeral. The hard erection and its emission are at hand, here and now, then gone, their return unpredictable and never totally assured, more absent than present. The girl knows her body as evolving toward palpable encounter with the mysteries of life; the boy feels his palpable encounter with these mysteries dwindle and become remote. The female's cycles are predictable, the man's capricious. The prized gift, the emblem of manhood, it turns out after all, is not given to him to keep. The father's contribution to new life is done in a spurt, while the mother's burgeons, on and on, more and more noticeably.

The rhythms of life to which men are tuned by their sexuality are the rhythms of death and rebirth: Lose life to make it. That which most ultimately emblems maleness, the proudly erect phallus, is precisely what is forsaken for the sake of seeding new life. Women receive and burgeon. Men spend and surrender, surrender not just seed but tumescence, vitality, alertness. (In some species, the male's life itself is surrendered in the devouring that accompanies copulation.) Women are tuned to such periodicities as the rhythms of the moon and the cycles of fecundity. (That has allowed conventional wisdom to overgeneralize and claim *all* rhythms for women.) There is an important difference between recurrent *periodicities*, allied with the feminine and with birth, and the *alternations* of death and rebirth that are reclaimed here for the masculine. The recurrent cycles of moon and menstruation suggest a completeness, a promise, a fulfillment that is quite distinguishable from death–rebirth alternations, which suggest the harsher realities (and perhaps larger promises) of "lose your life to save it." Although there is, to be sure, a waning and waxing of moon phases and of a woman's fertility, there is not the harsh dynamic that a "death" is *required* to make way for a renewed "life." (There is, of course, a kind of death in a woman's unfertilized ovum and its sloughing, but this *follows*, not allows, the openness to life and is preempted by fertilization and new life.)

So what we learn from our early genital sexuality is this: That which most makes us men also makes us strangers to ourselves, chronically wanting. Phallus and ejaculation and begetting, the most defining entities of manhood, are fugitive and temporary, unreliable and uncontrollable, insistent and resistant, as though with an independent will. That with which I especially need an experience of being one instead forces on me an experience of being at odds, a distance that feels, first of all, a distance from self. No wonder men at the core assume scarcity, unreliability, disjunction, displacement. No wonder men live by what is to come, tugged by promises that leave us rashly impatient and sullenly waiting. But making the promise come true is uphill and unlikely because all this dis-ease seems to be inflicted on me by creation; it is not derived from social or cultural norms or aberrations. What makes me male makes me dis-eased, hungrily hopeful.

Divided from Life

We are not done yet with anatomic differences. We have said that young boys and girls (extending into our lifelong childhood) notice that boys have something, anatomically, that girls do not. And we have noted that adolescent boys (extending into our lifelong adolescence) are preoccupied with the phallus they possess, but unreliably and uncontrollably. It may be that as we grow out of these preoccupations and move toward adulthood, men and women become growingly impressed with what females have and males don't: the capacity to give birth and to suckle. Much has been written about "womb envy"; it seems often as foolish or belligerent as a lot of writing about "penis envy." Sometimes all of men's assertiveness and aggressiveness is attributed not to their own hormones but, in effect, to relentless compensation for organs and hormones they lack.

Such adult envies are harder to track because adults are good at hiding feelings of this kind. But let us probe experience a bit. Last time you chanced on a woman nursing a baby, if you are a man, you probably averted your eyes and shuffled off the scene. Was this simply modesty or chivalry or taboo against looking? Perhaps. To be more psychoanalytic, could it have been a kind of anxiety triggered by a momentary temptation to identify with the baby and regress to the breast yourself? Perhaps. Or could it have been connected, unconsciously, to some primitive desire to be like that mother? It would be a desire so absurd, so out of reach, so unmanly that it would trigger anxiety, avoidance, suppression, averted eyes. The impossibility of such a wish is as absolute a biological barrier around male existence as death is a limit on all life. Confronting a nursing woman may, paradoxically, be like confronting a corpse, because both encounters are face-to-face confrontations with a man's own mortality, with a man's apprehension of his unwanted but unavoidable separation from life. In the vocabulary of this book, the encounter leaves him with a sense of primordial sorrow.

Are similar reactions possible to an encounter with pregnancy? Are you comfortable around a pregnant woman, or ill at ease? Does pregnancy seem, somehow, a forbidden holy domain, an inner sanctuary from which you are excluded without hope of appealing for access? Is life-giving experienced as a taboo for men? Does a man especially "want" what he is fated never to possess?

What about encounter with birth itself? In most cultures, the exclusion of fathers from the act of birth has been ratified by literal physical separation. Now that men are admitted, physically, to the birthing room and invited to participate, does it *feel* comfortable? Or is there an undercurrent of dis-ease, "I don't belong here"? Some fathers still stand by, awkward and adjunct. Others express their discomfort by trying to take charge, coaching the mother and second-guessing the doctor. Is it uncomfortable to be "merely" assisting and witnessing and yielding the actual birth unambiguously to the woman? We can't be precise, but it does seem likely that, at some primitive level, men are aware of an irremediable deficit that is their lot as men, some unbridgeable separation from life, rawly and plainly experienced.

Man Alone

Beyond anatomy, manhood is shaped by a crucial happening in almost every boy's experience in almost every culture. There comes a time in a young boy's life when he must make a move to claim identity as a male. He must separate from intimate connection with his mother.[1] He must go his own way and become different from her if he is to be a man. But, it turns out, the move seems to have the profound side effect of requiring him to feel unbridgeably separated from the sources and signs of life itself—sidelined and wanting, in the language of this chapter. The same formative influence that makes men men makes men feel deficient. This influence is not as fixed and inevitable as anatomy but may, nevertheless, be nearly inevitable and nearly universal, as universal as the child-rearing circumstance that it is the mother who gives primary care to the infant. It is the mother who gives and symbolizes life to the infant boy, and it is the mother from whom he must devise a dramatic separation, for the sake of his own maleness. To become male he must separate from life as he knows it.

Consider, as developmentalists[2] have considered in recent years, this difference between the ways that boys and girls must relate to their mother, especially in the formative preschool years. Something like this, subject of course to many

1. The conventional Freudian analysis plays the separation drama differently but with the same effect. The boy must abandon intimate connection with his mother because it competes with his father's intimate connection with her. The boy must yield to the father to avoid the father's displeasure and to preserve the father as mentor, model, and ally in becoming a man.
2. The best summary is by Lillian B. Rubin, *Intimate Strangers: Men and Women Together* (New York: Harper & Row, 1983).

23

variations, seems to be the basic developmental scenario: Girls have the advantage that their primary caregiver (and life-giver) can be their primary role model. They know they are to grow up female, and to learn how to do that—how to behave and feel and think of themselves as female—they have both model and encouragement at hand in the person they are already closest to and dependent on. In adolescence, of course, to forge independent identity, it becomes necessary to pull away from this tight connection. But for the purpose of learning to think of oneself as female in these earliest years, it is comfortable and natural to honor and strengthen the connection and identification that already exists between mother and child into an identification between mother and daughter. The little girl follows unambiguously and comfortably, even clings to her mother and mimics her caretaking, her mannerisms on the telephone, and much else.

For a boy it is not that easy. He knows he is to grow up male, and he also recognizes early on that to achieve this he must not honor and strengthen but disrupt the bonds between himself and his primary caregiver, his life-giver. There may or may not be a father readily at hand to become the model for maleness, but the young boy does recognize that his mother is not the right model and he must distance himself from her, sometimes rejecting her clumsily, sometimes striking out with exaggerated independence, sometimes more smoothly and happily. But it is not easy. She has genuinely been the source and symbol of life itself. It is not too strong to say that the young boy is forced to choose between maleness and connectedness with life. The normal choice is for maleness, but this leaves a residual chasm, lifelong, between self and life, a chasm the man experiences as inherent part of his maleness.

This simple, obvious difference between growing up a boy and growing up a girl seems to have profound and lasting effects. Many characteristic differences between men and women result from the difference between a boy's need to put distance between himself and his mother and the girl's requirement to stay close. Women seem primed by this experience to build bridges, men to build boundaries. Women favor relationships, connections, syntheses, between people as between ideas. Men tend to stay aloof from relationship; they analyze, compartmentalize, emphasize distinctions and differences, whether among ideas or people. Sometimes this penchant for distinctions generates comparison or rivalry, sometimes a scheme of hierarchy; it may be that these two infamous qualities of men—competitiveness and hierarchical preferences—are rooted mainly in this proclivity for distinctions. Rivalry and hierarchy reinforce and guarantee the importance of things being one thing and not something else, an urgency and a habit generated by the boy's need to be not like mother so he can be male. Rivalry and hierarchy, sometimes dubbed as compensation or cover-up for a male sense of weakness or a "fragile ego," are perhaps more accurately regarded as side effects of this transaction of male identity-building that leave an inevitable wound, the haunting feeling that something essential is missing, that being male costs a connectedness with life.

There is also the characteristic of male self-reliance, the much advertised, much vaunted, much demeaned, much misunderstood self-sufficiency and independence of men. It is apparent how a self-reliance, even self-centeredness, emerges out of the male-vs.-mother dilemma just described. If dependence on mother and connectedness with mother appear too threatening to male identity, they must be renounced; to be safe, so must *all* dependence and connectedness. Women weave webs, but a man must rely on himself. For women, scarcity and deficit—and rescue from scarcity and deficit—tend to lie outside, in relationship with others. When something feels missing, it is connection with another. For men, scarcity and deficit—and remedy—lie within, in self. When something feels missing, it is a part of the self.[3]

We have seen that conventional wisdom attributes to men a fragile ego, or insecurity, and a need to protect or hide or undo this frailty in a penchant for bluster, swagger, control, and other exaggerations of selfhood. This appraisal is conventionally made in the spirit of moral accusation or psychiatric diagnosis: This is how men are flawed. Here we say simply: This is how men *are*. Or perhaps: This is how men come to recognize

---

3. The difference must be similar to the distinction often drawn between shame and guilt. Guilt is rooted in residue or apprehension of the judgment of others, the breaking of connection. Shame has to do with a sense of emptiness or defectiveness of the self.

how humans beings are. "Fragile ego" is a petty approximation of the profound perplexities, the precariousness of the human predicament and its promise, that men come to apprehend. The male's avenues of discovery tracked here are not distortions but means of revelation. This is how men learn that life is chronically destined, beset by expectancy, and how men learn to thrive in that plight and to trust its promises.

Adam and Oedipus
as Epitomes of Manhood

3

Adam

"Therefore the Lord God sent him forth from the garden of Eden, to till the ground from which he was taken. He drove out the man; and at the east of the garden of Eden he placed the cherubim, and a sword flaming and turning to guard the way to the tree of life." (Gen. 3:23–24). So ends the Bible's account of Adam's initiation into manhood.

Exiled

Adam is to live under curse. He is to live exiled from the locus and livelihood for which he was created and destined; he is cordoned off from the tree of life itself. The separation is absolute, unchallengeable, enforced by mysterious suprahuman powers, barriers he cannot even fathom, much less overcome; he can only submit. He is destined ineffably not to live his destiny.

Most poignant, Adam is forced to "to till the ground from which he was taken." At the beginning of the story God created Adam by raising him up out of the ground (Gen. 2:7). Now Adam finds himself reworking that same ground. He has lived "from dust to dust"—the language of burial. At the core of his curse, Adam cannot take his creation for granted and move on. He is sentenced to endless working and reworking the stuff of his own being—in Hebrew, "man" and "ground" are puns on each other—replowing old ground, like perpetual therapy, perpetual growing up, perpetual pilgrimage, never settled, never arrived. It feels like the deepest circle of hell, creatures forced forever to keep reworking their own formation, from the ground up. But the Bible says this is a man's life: unending adolescence, unending midlife crisis, reexamining goals and identities and priorities, and reexamining again, constantly recycling the substance of his life through its seasons. A man's ground of being apparently is less like a sure foundation than like shifting sands.

Just when a man sees a light at the end of the tunnel, it recedes and dims. Just when relations with his teenage kids seem to have stabilized and the rules for living together as a family seem ready to work, just when he feels he's managed the right balance of empathy and firmness, a new adolescent urgent experimentation breaks out and it's back to square one. Just when tensions on the job have been faced and some balance worked out between the way the boss wants things done and you do, the boss changes. Just when the budget balances or a balance of household responsibilities seems reached with your spouse and you're ready to leave that fretting behind and move on, it's off balance again. All that ground to be reworked, bogged down in getting ready to live, never getting on with it. Like spending a lifetime assembling the tools and materials for a woodworking project, or drawing blueprints, never allowed to move beyond. All windup and no pitch. Endless tumescence.

All we are told about Adam after his exile is that he lived for 930 years!—perhaps a way of making vivid how virtually unending is the task of tilling and retilling the ground of one's being—and that he started a family. Not another word about those 930 years. It's as though we are to picture, as prototype of a man's life, nearly a millennium of dutiful uneventful domestic tedium, all in the shadow of the guarded gates of an Eden intended to be home but in fact an alien bastion, never claimed.

Not only does the biblical account give this testimony to men's sorrow and alienation, these chapters of Genesis also try to account for this alienation. We have to make comprehensible and palpable what is otherwise vivid but unfathomable, that experience of living out of reach of one's own identity and destiny. The barrier is baffling and formidable. We are locked out of our selves by something beyond our own doing, beyond our own fathom or control. Women speak of a "glass ceiling," that invisible barrier they slam into when trying to reach into positions of greater responsibility and authority. For men, not so much denied promotion and recognition as denied "getting a life," it feels more like a glass cage. No, it feels more like the fiercer imagery of the Bible. The Creator has slammed the gates and set a guard, "cherubim, and a sword flaming and turning." But why?

Why can't I reap from the tree of life? Why can't I just claim my destiny, we secretly cry out, or not so secretly lunge out. Why can't I find meaning, fullness, yes-ness in my work, my parenting, my love life, my retirement years?

Stunted

The conventional understanding of the Genesis account of "why" has it as punishment for misdeed, for disobedience and rebellion, prideful overreaching. This conventional understanding casts Adam and Eve as naughty children disobeying rules set by their Better. They have been provided a comfortable home, but the provider has set limits. God tells Adam, "You may freely eat of every tree of the garden," except. . . ! Not the tree of knowledge or the tree of life. The account does not claim that the limits are wise or benign or necessary; God does not say to Adam, "These rules are for your own good." They are presented in the story as arbitrary limits, perhaps even self-serving for God, to protect his own status. God makes a power issue out of possession of knowledge. The limitation is less like a father saying, You can't drive my car because it's dangerous for you, than, You can't drive my car because it's my car. What, after all, turned out to be the effect of crossing the line and eating the forbidden fruit? They did not die; the snake had been right about that, and God had been deceptive. Rather, "the eyes of both were opened, and they knew that they were naked" (Gen. 3:7a). Their act yielded understanding and self-knowledge: hardly dire or disastrous consequences. Hardly too much to aspire to for a human being, a creature endowed and blessed as richly as was Adam in these Genesis accounts. Genesis 1:26 quotes God, "Let us make humankind in our image, according to our likeness." To be a godlike human being is, of course, to aspire to knowledge, self-consciousness, and life. Eating of the

29

tree of knowledge is, in a most profound sense, doing what comes naturally. To try to forbid such fruit is to frustrate and deny the very qualities that make a human being human. It's a cosmic tease.

Conventional interpretation, as it often does, has tended to sexualize the events in the garden and the forbidden fruit and to cast the "sin" of Adam (and Eve) as sexual trespass. If there is warrant for such interpretation, it is in the report that, before the eating of the fruit, "the man and his wife were both naked, and were not ashamed" (Gen. 2:25) and that afterward "they knew that they were naked; and they sewed fig leaves together and made loincloths for themselves" (Gen. 3:7b); also in the fact that Genesis recounts sexual relations between the two only after the eating of the fruit. But this sounds less like sexual trespass and more like sexual maturation. If being created human implies a legitimate aspiration for full knowledge, so too does being created human imply a legitimate potential for full sexual development and self-awareness. If this is what Adam (and Eve) aspired to and attained, this was not distortion. The distortion and the distress—the sorrow—occurred in the paradox with which they were taunted in the garden: They were denied the fulfillment of the (sexual) potential with which they were created. If there is an issue of sexuality in the Genesis account, this is it, in exact parallel to the issue of hunger for knowledge.

So the scene in the garden portrays the same plight as the scene, in exile, outside it: Adam and Eve, where she also appears in the account, are profoundly teased. They are living in the shadow of their destiny, even in the garden, even before eating the fruit, before exile, before a flaming sword bars the way. What it's like to be in the garden of Eden, according to this story, is to be endowed with aspirations that reach beyond what is allowed. It's to be spiritually stunted.

Incomplete

Yet the motif of chronic yearning pervades the story of Adam even earlier. From his beginning, from the moment of his creation, Adam is portrayed as experiencing an incompleteness.[1]

1. Of the two creation stories in Genesis, the first (Gen. 1:1–2:4a) regards men and women in fully equal ways. There is no mention of male that is not joined by mention of female, just as there is no mention of individual

When Adam finds himself in the garden of Eden, as Genesis tells it, he is in the midst of abundant and lush life. He is in paradise. But there is no mention of joy, no contentment or delight, no thanksgiving—for the bliss, for the completeness and wonder of all creation, or for Adam's abiding place in it. Instead, the experience is *Is that all there is?* Adam is *created* as a man of sorrow.

The story is insistent about the lushness: four rivers flowing abundantly, "every tree that is pleasant to the sight and good for food," every imaginable creature at his bidding. Adam is at home in Eden, with good work to do and its fruits to enjoy. But the story is insistent, too, about the discontent. The prevailing mood apparently is *Something's missing.* Adam is in want. Adam is alienated from the wholeness of his life. This is the mood God senses and addresses, enriching Adam's garden still more with a parade of new creatures offered to him as candidates to be a suitable companion. The God who has pronounced all creation good in *his* eyes, recognizes incompleteness when he sees things through the eyes of the man.

Finally, a companion appears to be found to Adam's satisfaction, a woman. But this is done in a peculiar way, at the sacrifice of wounding a portion of his own body—as though the symbolism is careful to make the point that the deficiency can only be exchanged or replaced, never fully remedied. Adam now has a mate, but he is short a rib, new badge of unending incompleteness.[2]

Re-deeming "Original Sin"

"Sin" is perhaps the word that Western culture has most used to identify the experience of wrongness and distortion

persons, no Adam or Eve. "So God created humankind in his image . . . male and female he created them." (Gen. 1:27). Correspondingly, the first story is without the motifs of tease and yearning recounted here. Life is blessed ("God blessed them, and God said to them 'Be fruitful and multiply . . . and have dominion . . . over every living thing.'" Gen. 1:28), not withheld or cursed. It is the second story, beginning at Genesis 2:4b, in which Adam is the principal character, which portrays the tensions and travails recounted here—as though they are especially connected with the lot of the individual male. It seems that a story that sets out to give an account of the creation of a man finds itself portraying a chronic yearning.

2. Perhaps the same point is made by immediately portraying this woman, a satisfying companion, as an agent in the events leading to eviction from the garden. It is tempting to linger on this aspect of the Adam and Eve story,

recounted in these opening chapters of the Bible. If we adopt that word to label our alienation, we need to be careful not to impose a modern-day notion of moralism into both this term and this account. This is not the relatively trivial notion of sins as misdeeds, violations of morality or duty or commitment. And we need to be careful not to impose a tragic or dualistic sense of an "evil" imposed on us; Job deals with that. Rather, the accounts of Adam, as a kind of prototypical man, deal with the conviction of a more primordial, entrenched, relentless flaw, a wrongness and an alienation that is a part of one's endowment—not simply an error of one's "doings" (or the evil of another's doings) but a fundamental flaw of one's very "being." It's part of us from the beginning, original sin. It can't be righted by any earthly means but only, if at all, by the mysteries of extraordinary transcendent intervention. So meanwhile, in the only life we know, it is to be lived with. If we say we live in sin, it is not that we do wrong or are wronged; the truth is that we *are* wrong.

Unlike the conventional wisdom that readily supposes that Adam's—and our—yearning and alienation is a consequence of misdeed, in the reading here, the yearning and alienation—the sorrow—is part of creation, and God has deemed all creation good! So let us also deem this part of creation as good: Adam, as all men, is made that way—to live in the shadow of his destiny, in the vocabulary of this book—and it is a welcome trait, to be lived not just with courage, certainly not with resigned stoicism, but with pride and eagerness and confidence: to be lived in expectancy. No regrets or recrimination, no assigning

that in Adam's view the woman is the solution to his problems and then immediately the cause of his problems. "At last," he sighs (Gen. 2:23), as he welcomes her to his side, presaging the sigh of every man who, in longing or in person, relies on a woman to bring him surcease and identity, to assuage the emptiness. But then he blames her for his predicament, regarding her as something imposed on him. ("The man said, 'The woman whom you gave to be with me, she gave me fruit from the tree'" [Gen. 3:12.]) It is a temptation much succumbed to, to suppose that it is a woman who solves a man's problems or brings them about. In much literature about men these days, this takes one of two forms: (1) It is often supposed that the problems men have to deal with these days result from changes women are making in their own lives; the challenge, it is often said, is how to live with the "liberated" woman or with "feminism." (2) It is often supposed that the solution for men is to adopt allegedly feminine traits, like "sensitivity" or "vulnerability"; the challenge is said to be to become more like a woman. These temptations are resisted in this book.

of blame, no illusions about living beyond it, no programs for getting over the sorrow, outgrowing it, or curing it. Man's sorrow is a constructive ingredient for man's life. A man's sorrow is his hope. This is the platform for the chapters that follow.

Adam's blunder, his misdeed, is the *consequence* of his sorrow, his sense of incompleteness, not the cause of it, as conventional interpretation would have it in supposing that all was well in Eden until the tasting of forbidden fruit and that men create their own misery. In claiming the apple, Adam was lunging to assuage his spiritual hunger, and the error was in the lunging, the seizing, not in the hungering. The man who tries to command the affection of his children is not, first of all, creating alienation from his children—though his commanding posture certainly enhances it. He is, first of all, *revealing* that alienation, in his blustering attempt to undo it. When a woman tries to share some misgivings and a man responds with muteness or bland formulaic reassurance, he is, first of all, in this insensitive silencing or silence, expressing the inadequacy he feels in the encounter and, second, trying to seize a solution, to master the sorrow. We can regret the clumsy tactic and find it futile, and self-defeating, but we must also recognize the motive, the hunger that invents it.

To see Adam, foremost, as sinner, to blame the "fall" for the sorrow, is to blame the symptom as the cause.[3] It is to suppose

3. Of the many reasons we seem predisposed to regard Adam primarily as sinner and to blame him for our own sense of exile from the good life, one seems worth noting here. To blame Adam as the sinner who has left us cursed echoes and focuses one of the ways—perhaps a prominent way— each of us thinks of his own father: the spoiler. He is the figure who had the chance to make his (and our own) life great. He—we—could have lived in paradise. But he was too clumsy, or too wrongheaded, or too heedless, or too reckless, or too blundering, or too unaware, maybe too selfish, maybe too easily led around, and he blew it, ruined it for himself and for us. He screwed up, this father whose distortions of life are imposed on his sons. He is the cause of our sorrow. Adam is that father who is fundamentally disappointed and disappointing. In Christian theology, this father's trespass leaves it to the Son to try to repair, and the trespass is so great its repair demands sacrificial action by the Son. That story is lodged in every son's imagination/memory—that urge, at whatever cost, to rescue his mother or his family or his own destiny from the disappointing father; to undo, with our own sorrow, the sorrow he inflicts and perhaps the sorrow he suffers. To be father of the human race is to be the spoiler, even the abuser, of what could have been, the one whose exile from life-as-promised causes us to be exiled too. That's how we have come to project on Adam.

that men are first abusive and manipulative and distortive of life and then, as a result, feel alienated, in sorrow. It is like regarding men only as villains, not victims in their own way, like regarding men by their outward doings, not their inward yearnings. Or it is like regarding God (the Father) by his outward doings, trying to solve the calculus of his mercy and his severe expectations as though the mercy and the expectations were somehow the essential components of Godhead, without regarding the sorrow that *is* at the heart of Godhead and at the heart of both mercy and severe expectation.

Oedipus

Sigmund Freud has made the tragic Greek figure of Oedipus the emblem and epitome of the male experience, the prototypical man in his canon, as Adam is in the biblical canon. The "Oedipus complex" becomes, for Freud and for many of us, the kernel of male identity. But if we accept Freud's intuition that we understand our maleness more clearly when we see ourselves as Oedipus, we should take care to know Oedipus more completely, more honestly, than what Freud chose to describe.

There is much more to the Oedipus story and to our story than Freud told us—or, more accurately, more than he *consciously* told us. There is ample reason to suppose, as we shall see, that Freud was drawn to this tragic figure and identified with him, as he asked us each to identify with him, precisely for what is portrayed in that part of the story he did *not* tell us. After all, if we are to believe Freud's own principles, the part of a story not told is the most important part, the most revealing. A fixation as strong as that which Freud lodged on Oedipus most likely suggests intense unconscious energies.

The Legend

Here, in brief, is the Greek legend of Oedipus. He was born son to Laius, king of Thebes, and his wife Jocasta. When Laius learned from an oracle that he was destined to be killed by his son, he took the preemptive precaution of ordering the newborn abandoned on a mountainside. But the baby was rescued by a passing shepherd and raised by a foster father, whom

Oedipus thought to be his natural father. So when the adult Oedipus heard the same oracle, that he was destined to kill his father, he took the honorable precaution of leaving home. On his travels he encountered Laius as a stranger on the road, quarreled with him, and killed him. Continuing his travels, he came to Thebes, which he found tormented by the Sphinx, whose tyranny he dispelled by answering the Sphinx's riddle. The city rewarded him by making him king and husband of Jocasta. Many years and several children later, Oedipus learned the truth and, in his horror, blinded himself. He is portrayed in his old age, blinded and crippled, cared for by his loyal daughter Antigone.

The Interpretation

Freud plucked from this story the fact that Oedipus killed his father and married his mother, as though this were done knowingly rather than out of the best of intentions and ignorance, and he assigned Oedipus' name to a boy's deliberate but unconscious desires to do the same.

Freud's one-sided portrayal of Oedipus is the same as the conventional one-sided portrayal of Adam: He is an offender. It also matches the one-sided disparaging portrayal of men often preferred by the conventional wisdom of our time. Oedipus (like Adam and many a contemporary man) is known only as a villain, a wrongdoer, a relentless achiever, abuser, overreacher, power-hungry exploiter: testosterone run amok. The Oedipus within each man is said to name the villainous part of him, a sober warning of just how far "macho" can go if left untethered, competitive to the point of killing even one's father, exploitative of women to the point of claiming even one's mother. He is not known as the victim of abandonment and abuse, which he was, nor as the intrepid pilgrim in earnest and conscientious pursuit of his own destiny, which he also was.

What Freud told us, like Sophocles before him and like conventional discussion today of men, was about Oedipus in tragic and titanic midlife distress. Oedipus was content and thriving, as husband, as father, as king—everything at home and at work going well—when he discovered that things were not as they seemed; he was on a detour from his own life. But Freud left out (ironically, for one who insisted so sternly on the defining power of childhood) what Homer and the folk stories had told so dramatically about the childhood events that set the midlife tragedy into motion. Freud, like so much conventional discussion today about men, told us about the wrongs the adult Oedipus inflicted, but nothing about the wrongs inflicted on the child Oedipus. Freud told us about Oedipus the imposter, but nothing about Oedipus the deceived. Freud told us about Oedipus destructively driven and ambitious, but nothing about Oedipus abandoned and helplessly vulnerable.

The full story, which was long withheld from Oedipus (and which, it seems, Freud still wants to withhold from us, in concert with the contemporary critique of masculinity that focuses on men's damaging midlife doings), tells how these disastrous and destructive happenings came to be. It tells how tragedy was inflicted on Oedipus, not fashioned by him.

Oedipus is not villain but victim, a man who spent most of his life in exile, on the run, on a pilgrimage in search of himself, but was denied his own life, the epitome of life lived in the shadow of its own destiny. Fate inflicted tragedy on Oedipus despite his best intentions and commitment. The life he thought he was living was not his life at all and was snatched from him. His own life was withheld from him, behind an impenetrable veil, until it surfaced in violent eruption. "Oedipus complex" should be the name for our existential vulnerability, for our most soulful and excruciating wanting, for those raw moments when a man finds himself dispossessed of his own life. Oedipus personifies the discovery that a man's life collides with limits he doesn't expect, doesn't comprehend, doesn't deserve, and can't do anything about. *Something*—which may be the key to the whole thing—*is missing*. My life as I know it is smaller than it really is. *Is that all there is?* Oedipus teaches us to wonder. But with the warning, *Ask at your own risk!*

All Freud told us, consciously, was about Oedipus as victimizer. But there is no Oedipus story, there is no Oedipus as victimizer and villain, without Oedipus first abandoned and Oedipus duped, Oedipus unwitting imposter, Oedipus in want, Oedipus barred (even as you and I) from living his own life fully and freely, Oedipus conscripted into living out a script that was not his choice and not him. The Oedipus story is nothing if not the most painful portrait imaginable of a man separated from his own life in ways he but dimly senses and slowly discovers.

Oedipus is nothing if not a pilgrim, twice compelled to renounce home and settled life, by his conviction that life at home
is beset by wrongness and that remedy lies abroad. What Freud
left out is the part that connects with our experience of our own
life.

Denying Manly Sorrow

Freud told us about Oedipus the way men's stories are usually told. Conventional analysis of the male experience, including much abuse we inflict on ourselves, usually starts in the
middle, the way Freud's (and Sophocles') account of Oedipus
does. (Since this is often especially true of the feminist perspective on the male experience, it is ironic to find Freud, usually the bane of feminists, in this company.) The conventional
analysis starts with a man enacting a script of control or dom-
ination or even violence, a man desperately trying to save his
own life barehanded. To be conventional, this book should skip
these early chapters, portraying men in sorrow. It should open
with analysis that is to come later, which will deplore the destructive strategies men often adopt, preferring, for example, to
become colonists or crusaders rather than pilgrims, to play the
role of monarch rather than magi, to aspire to an undue pater-
nalism rather than delight in the expectancy of being a son. But
we can understand these deflections more truly, as we can understand Oedipus more truly, when we see them in the context
of the sorrows here recounted.

How perverse for Freud to make Oedipus the symbol for
wanting to murder one's father. That's the one thing Oedipus
did *not* want to do. Oedipus wanted much, above all else a father who would deal honestly and responsibly with him. But
Oedipus decidedly did not want to kill his father.

Far from wanting to murder his father, Oedipus did everything he could to avoid it. Far from wanting to murder his father, his father wanted to murder him. Far from wanting to
murder his foster father, he only needed for the man to tell him
the truth. Far from intending to transgress the taboo against incest, he was the victim of a taboo against truth and full disclo-
sure. Far from being guilty of immorality, he was too duped by
betrayal and deception to be capable of responsible moral
choice.

Much of Freud's career was haunted and energized by the dilemma of distinguishing intentions (or wishes) from acts. Which is disguise and which is genuine? Which is primary and which is derived? For example, he flipflopped on the question of whether women's accounts of abuse and incest were likely to be accurate reports of events or expressions of unconscious fantasy; on balance he concluded emphatically for the priority and power of inner motives and taught us all how these can drive behavior and memory of behavior. So it seems particularly notable that in this case of the Oedipus story, Freud, the apostle of the authority of the inner life, should ignore evidence of intention and suppose that the objective events of patricide and incest can be equated with inner wishes. Such a fumbling departure from his own principles must have been required by some pressing inner need of Freud's own. Did Freud feel so keenly the pain of Oedipus' experience of abandonment and vulnerability that he could not acknowledge its power, either in Oedipus' life or his own?

If we turn to Freud's self-disclosing encounter with Oedipus to guide our own, we need to pay most attention to what Freud did *not* say. We can infer from Freud's silence that the most compelling part of the story for him, as probably for us, was Oedipus' vulnerability and plaintive search ever on the cusp of his own identity.

Freud as Oedipus

Perhaps Freud was drawn to the Oedipus story, of all stories, as the story of his own life just because he knew, so desperately, from his own infancy to old age, what it was to be in this kind of sorrow. If so, for the same reasons, of course, he had to leave that part of it untold. And if so, this is where it is most important to explore and to learn from Freud, to try to track his identification with Oedipus. Freud's fixation on Oedipus is, on his own terms, an invitation to probe. It is not trespassing or intrusive to accept that invitation. It is a way of learning more about ourselves by learning more of what Freud must have perceived in Oedipus.

More than once Freud explicitly identified himself with Oedipus. Freud the puzzler over riddles in the human psyche consciously identified with Oedipus the solver of the Sphinx's riddle—he once fantasized that his epitaph would honor him as Oedipus' successor in this regard. As the aging Freud, more and more pained and crippled by cancer and infirmities of sight, hearing, and speech, leaned on his faithful daughter Anna, he named her his Antigone—making himself the blinded, lamed, and chagrined Oedipus. And, of course, Freud most consciously identified with Oedipus caught in a romantic triangle with parents: Freud, whose entire life was animated by rivalrous and bitter competition with both mentors and disciples—fathers and sons—Freud, who lived three quarters of a century in the same household with the beautiful strong-willed woman who was his mother, while preserving an awkward, awed silence about her. So Freud saw himself as Oedipus the riddle solver, as Oedipus caught in romantic triangle with parents, and as Oedipus the aged invalid.

But, tellingly, Freud did not tell us about the infant Oedipus abandoned on the hillside, the foundling Oedipus raised by parents who were not his real parents, the youthful Oedipus betrayed by misinformation into tragically fateful blunders. By this silence we are invited to recall the toddler Freud storming through the house, throwing open cupboards, howling all the while, in frantic search for a mother who had forsaken him to give birth to another; or the child Freud repeating the scene when his beloved nanny was evicted from the household overnight without warning or farewell; or the young Freud discovering that life choices were limited for him, in ways not quite fathomable, by the vagaries of Viennese anti-Semitism; or the youthful Freud shaken in disillusionment when his father confessed submitting to anti-Semitic abuse on the streets. ("What did you do when they knocked your hat into the gutter?" "I picked it up.")

We are also invited by the silence to surmise, not without hints and evidence, the other dismaying moments and moods: when marriage proved far less enamoring than imagined and wanted, when professional collegial relationships were found wanting, when protégés defected, when children disappointed, when insights and theories proved intransigent and could not be wrestled into the clarity or completeness the scientist knew they possessed but kept hidden, when patients resisted and sloughed off the insights even once they were clear and correct.

But, finally, the story outruns either recall or surmise, just as psychology—"soul knowledge"—outruns biography or history and as the Oedipus tale carries its meaning quite apart from historical events or personalities at Thebes or in Vienna. What happened *to* Freud is of less moment than how he *experienced* it, the myths he found himself living inside. And there surely lodged Oedipus, epitome of the dislodged, disenchanted, displaced, destined life.

We are invited, too, by our own murkiness about such events in our own history to recall and surmise and experience what it is for us that is evoked by contemplating Oedipus the abandoned infant, Oedipus the son who was not a son, Oedipus from whom crucial lifesaving information was withheld, and Oedipus finally confronting in devastating, blinding horror the immensity of how far removed his life had become from what he thought it was.

Five Men

4

Alan:
Still in Pursuit of Father

"I'm going to have back out of our weekend." Alan is on the phone to Mark. "I got this letter from Dad today that just doesn't make any sense, and when I tried to call him tonight he makes less sense. So I've got to run up there Saturday and see what's going on. He's talking about ripping out all the shrubbery around his place and putting in sod. At least I think that's what he's talking about. He acts like I should know all about it, keeps saying I warned him about ticks, and I never heard of any of this. I hate it. But when he talked about swapping cars last winter and I didn't follow up on it, you know how he screwed that up."

Alan, Mark, and Will have been planning a weekend camping outing for months—well, years, actually. It had been all talk—it seemed like their only talk when the families got together for picnics—and nature magazine browsing, until Shirley said bluntly, "Why don't you just do it?" So they have a cooler already packed, and fishing gear, some out of the garage and some out of a catalog, and a campsite reserved by the river in the state park. And Alan feels OK about leaving the back porch unpainted one more week (just as it went unpainted all last summer while he spent Saturdays coaching the YMCA soccer team).

But he can't let his father's quirks go unattended. That's the main reason—his father's quirks and her mother's health—that he and Shirley have stopped talking about their dream trip to Spain. Both boys are out of the house now, and there is some hope of getting their education paid for. "Finally it's time for our honeymoon," they said. But now they have stopped collecting brochures. They mutter about exchange rates and terrorism, but it is clear they wouldn't feel right about going that far away from their parents.

Alan dreads what's ahead—he's seen it in his friends' lives—trying to take care of his father's failing health by phone and commuting; arranging for home health care and then a nursing home; moving his father, closing the house, disposing of truckfuls of stuff, managing money—his father resisting all the way. Alan has seen this all around him, but he's also pretended it couldn't happen to him. This was to be the time in his life saved for something else, saved for him. The kids are grown, the house is in good repair and almost paid for, the job seems secure, the marriage is comfortable. The word "grown-up" comes to mind. Everything has been a scramble uphill, but now he's there and ready to stop scrambling, ready to savor, when suddenly he's held hostage. His time, his choices, even his money, it may turn out, are not his own.

But it's more than that, he tries to explain to Shirley; it's that his father is not his father, either. He's not the sturdy heroic wizard Alan always supposed him to be. He's not the friend Alan always wanted him to be. Part of the sense of relief of being grown-up, with the scrambling finished, was the expectation that he could deal with his father on a grown-up basis, man to man, adult to adult, and maybe finally become friends. He has lived a life his father approved of, so misgivings about that are unnecessary. He is a man in his own right, independent and accomplished. It should feel that way with his father, at last, but it doesn't. Here they are still battling—this time over shrubbery!—in a low-key power struggle: who's right, who's boss. Only this time it's his father who plays the unreasonable, irresponsible adolescent. When did they pass each other, going in opposite directions? Wasn't there a brief magic moment when they were on a par, maybe even close? No. Rivalry, jockeying, and power struggle have always been their way with each other. Alan likes to think of himself as someone who has moved beyond all this; it's disheartening to find otherwise.

Five Men

This seems to be a man's lot, a man's discontent. Shirley says it's different for her. She can recognize Alan's chagrin at feeling hostage, not in charge of his own life; women are all too experienced in contending with such hazards of dependency. But Alan's feeling that he is (still) being deprived of a father because of having to deal with the failing old man—that is not her feeling. Caring for her mother in failing health comes more easily for her as a woman because her relation with her mother has always (and comfortably) included a large component of such nurturing. She shares with Alan the practical inconveniences and demands on her time, but the way she is able to relate to her mother now is the way it has always been and the way she has wanted.

She admits to herself that her life will be simpler and freer after her mother dies; her life would be simpler now if her mother were dead. She can entertain such a thought openly, as a fact of life. Alan can't; it comes too close to the dangerously hostile thoughts that have always lingered in the shadows of his relation with his father. Alan's distance from his father imposes a distance from himself.

With Alan and his father it's awkward unacknowledged competition—and also wishing it weren't so, a wish equally awkward and unacknowledged. Conversations are polite but impatient, clipped, and indirect. They can argue about shrubbery and cars and sod, and about the best route to drive from one house to the other. His father can protest, "You shouldn't have come all that way just for this," and Alan can proffer the usual reassuring lie, "I wasn't doing anything else today anyway." But neither one can say, *I hate this.* And they can't say, *I want to be friends.* They bear the sorrow in secret, as men do, especially fathers and sons. Alan is not so unexpressive with his wife or his friends or his boss—even with his own sons, he would like to think—and somehow he had imagined it was getting better with his father. But there it is, the stark distance persisting. *Something is missing.*

How do we appraise Alan's mood? Older, masculinist conventional wisdom scolds Alan for being so timid and urges him into the fray, and his father too. "Men need to provide vigorous role models for each other. Decide what's best and do it. And don't give up a camping weekend to fret about it." Newer, feminist conventional wisdom scolds Alan for being so competitive and self-concerned. "Why can't you be more like Shirley and just calmly take care of your father?" Instead of either conventional option, we will take the sorrow and longing seriously as a fact of life, a fundamentally important fact. Alan's wishes—for a sturdy father, for a genuine relation with his father, and for a self liberated from such ambiguities and rivalries—such wishes are worthy wishes, and also futile. So the sorrow is noble and inevitable—and can be constructive.

Alan's longing is so fundamental and so urgent that it deserves to be thought of as religious. Alan is looking for a grounding in his relationship with his father, a grounding he has craved all his life, affirming and defining. He looks to his father, in sadness, for the reassurance that it seems only his father can give, and won't: the reassurance that Alan belongs to life, that he has a designated place in the scheme of things. Alan has tried all his life, desperately, to earn this assurance from his father, without success. Such a blessing can only be a gift, not a transaction. And it remains a gift ungiven. A religious purist can explain to Alan what he already knows too well, that in looking to his father as a god (as to a lesser degree he may also have looked to job success, soccer coaching, diligent home maintenance, spouse, sons, and others), he is looking to a false god, an idol, who can never provide this religious assurance. But such purist judgment—as usual—misses the point. Alan's hunger is of cosmic dimensions, even if his father isn't. Alan's pursuit of his father is an urgent and exalted enterprise, a religious enterprise. It deserves to be esteemed as such, and it deserves to be guided as such.

To think about Alan's dilemma in religious terms is to be open to strategies and wisdom not otherwise apparent or plausible. For example (to anticipate chapter 9) Alan might discover that his place in the universe *is* provided and warranted by his relationship with his father, not in the ways he expected but rather in the very chaotic yearning he experiences. This *is* what life fundamentally is like; Alan *is* part of it. There is meaning to the notion of "losing" one's life to find it. In the language of chapter 9, Alan can discover roots and identity in his sonship precisely *because* of sonship's torments and ambiguities, not in denial or in spite of them. Such a turbulent sonship discloses and accesses life's deepest realities and powers. In Christian terms, Alan may come to fathom and appropriate the understanding that Jesus' saving power is precisely as a son, in anguishes of sonship not unlike Alan's.

Carl:
Dreamer Unwelcomed

As Donna tells their minister about it, no one could be as irresponsible or as uncommunicative as Carl. But when she talks to her friends, they say things like, "That's nothing, you should see my husband. Men are like that. The books all say so too."

What are men like, according to this conventional wisdom? What is Carl like, according to Donna?

There was the puppy he brought home. Donna and Carl had talked about a dog several times and agreed that it would be good for the kids. But she hadn't made up her mind yet. "I'm the one who gets stuck cleaning the rug and lugging home bags of kibbles and settling arguments about who last walked the dog." ("Men just like to play and leave the work to us," her friend Alice agreed. "Like as soon as they get their sex, it's all over," Jean added. "They're so immature. He probably just wants the puppy for himself.")

The afternoon he appeared with the puppy, Donna exploded. "You don't listen to me, you don't talk to me, you don't care what I think! You don't care about the consequences of what you do. You just aren't responsible. You shoot from the hip without thinking and without looking at what you're doing. You don't care about any of the rest of us. You don't care about anything except what you suddenly take it in your head to do. It's not just the puppy. It's the trip you suddenly planned last spring, and it's taking the kids out for ice-cream cones the other night, just when I had them settled down ready for bed. And the cruising you do looking for a new house in neighborhoods you know we can't afford. I'm afraid some night you're going to bring home a new car, and we can't afford that either."

(In other households the conversation may be about the man's dream to open a restaurant or move to Vermont or take up windsurfing or get a new outdoor barbecue grill.)

Carl responded defensively. "But we did talk. You agreed that the dog would be great, as long as we all pitched in to help, and the kids and I have promised to do that. And you liked the trip last spring, and the kids went to bed happy after the ice-cream cones." So the battle, as usual with such defensive I-said-you-said exchanges, lingered unresolved. Donna and Carl, we all know, need to get down to talking about what really is happening between them.

But what *is* really happening? Power struggles between them? Probably. Carl's fear of being second-choice parent and needing to make a big gesture to woo his children? Probably. We can even escalate that diagnosis and suppose Carl is compensating for misgivings about his own masculinity (whatever that may mean to him or us: potency? authority? decisiveness?). Is the issue Donna's resentment over being confined to home and parenting while he enjoys the more active world, symbolized even by the opportunity—which he had in an ordinary day, and she didn't—to stop by the pet store and buy a dog? Probably. Any psychologist, amateur or professional, any friend, any reader can easily come up with many such surmises and insights that would fit and benefit Carl and Donna. (If only we could understand ourselves as astutely as we understand other people!) But, insightful and helpful as are such conventional surmises, they may not be complete.

Here is another interpretation of what may really be going on in this and similar battles. Carl is one who regards his life as en route, and Donna regards her life as arrived. What we have just overheard is (in the language of chapter 7) a conversation between a pilgrim and a homesteader. Of course they misunderstand, annoy, threaten, and fear each other. In what is a profound religious affirmation, whether he knows it that way or not, the pilgrim sees his life as fated for "more," as belonging beyond its visible boundaries, as lodged in a destiny that transcends and transforms the present. He is discontent with the here and now, not because it is unsatisfactory but because he trusts in something grander to break in or break out. He keeps probing the boundaries to discern that transcendence and let it in. Settling down, as though he had arrived, threatens to abort the promise he feels.

Carl does not want to abandon the family or disrupt it—as his moves feel to Donna. He wants it to become a better family. Donna does not want to frustrate his dreams and hopes—as he may feel it. She wants to anchor them. A pilgrim knows that the blessing is found afar, but also a pilgrim brings the blessing home; he doesn't take up residence at the distant shrine. A religious saving must always come from a realm beyond—Carl knows that—and it must always become fully lodged, incarnated in the immediate—Donna knows that. That-which-is-to-come and that-which-is must wholly heed each other. Carl and Donna need each other.

Puppies and ice-cream cones may be rash, trivial, or foolish ways to probe the transcendent for a transformed family life, but there is profound precedent and valid faith in risking trust in what seems foolish; whatever genuinely transforms must, by definition, appear misfit and foolish, radical. Saviors can save only when they come from a realm beyond. Grace never makes sense.

The error is not in risking a foolish experiment; the error is in mistaking the experiment for the solution. Carl's error comes anytime he gets overattached to a particular newness, whenever he may forsake the search with the claim, I found it: the puppy must stay, ice-cream cones every night. In language to come in later chapters, the dream becomes conscripted, the pilgrim becomes a colonist, the wise man becomes ally or servant to the monarch, the sacrament pointing to the transcendent becomes an idol pointing only to itself. Carl abandons his dream, his religious commitment to destiny-to-come, when he mistakes puppy or ice-cream cones for having arrived, when he substitutes a destination for living chronically destined.

If Donna and Carl would see themselves as different in this way—differing not in degree of commitment but in kind, not in degree of responsibility but in its form: pilgrim and homesteader—perhaps their different values and strategies and priorities might seem less obtuse, less arbitrary, less irksome, less like flaws, more natural, inevitable, acceptable, just different. Carl may not be the reckless irresponsible adolescent Donna sees. He may be just a pilgrim, questing beyond confining narrow horizons—which define home and family for her but which thwart home and family for him—questing for that freshness that, for him, promises to restore home and family and, for her, threatens to undo it. He may not be just an insensitive clod, not noticing or caring that he makes Donna's already tedious homemaking job more burdensome. He may genuinely and earnestly want to brighten that tedium and lighten the burden.

"You're always going for the dare," Donna complains, "stirring things up. You can't leave well enough alone." She's right about Carl, and she's right about herself. "Leaving well enough alone" *is* her way, and it is decidedly *not* Carl's. Of course his style makes her life miserable. Her energies are devoted to getting the family settled, smooth, in accord, coordinated, to getting schedules, and chores, and budgets designed and maintained. His energies are devoted to breaking out of just those confining routines of dailiness she finds so comfortable and necessary, to be open as a man of faith to that expected but unexpected miracle that will transform, uplift family life *out* of its settled but far from complete(d) patterns, the blessing that will restore that life to what it is meant to be. She's wrong to find sinister motives and to shout out, "You're only *trying* to make my life miserable." But we would be wrong not to realize that in this clash of styles they make each other miserable.

I want to say two things to Carl.

First, trust your discontent, which is to say, trust your faith. The dailiness *is* deadening, shackling, conserving family as a museum exhibit when it should be a joyful parade. "Things as they are" is just what is wrong, and what is called for is to discard the very dailiness that Donna seems to treasure. That dailiness is spinning its wheels, digging in deeper—endless and fruitless conversations and hand-wringing and sniping, low-grade chronic dysfunction. It is not centering but is destroying the center, the true meaning of "family" and all the things Donna (too) wants to preserve. There is more to marriage and family than protecting it from the disruption of getting a puppy. Honor your intuition of a need to transcend and transform dailiness.

Second, I would say to Carl, trust your discontent but not the particular solutions you find for it. Don't get stuck in new boundaries as confining as those you would transcend. There is more to marriage and family than delight in puppies and ice-cream cones too, so don't insist on them. Honor Donna's discontent with them, as you want your own discontent honored. In an alliance of discontents, move together and move on. The religious enterprise is always played with pieces that move off the board.

Howard:
Old and on Hold

The checkout clerk at the supermarket is confused. Howard can handle that; he knows how to wait patiently. The register readout says $16.72. He has given her a twenty, plus two dimes and two pennies; she owes him three singles and two quarters. This will give him some quarters for parking—one of the simple survival skills he relishes. He realizes he has outpaced this clerk for the moment, but he can wait for her to catch up. He will explain it to her if he has to. But better to let her punch it out on her keypad: *$20.22 received.* The computer will understand him and explain it to her: *$3.50 change.*

The trouble is, she doesn't know she is outpaced or confused. She thinks *he* is confused, and that is much harder for Howard to handle. He's used to being the savvy one, the person people turn to for solutions and answers. "How did you figure that out so quickly?" and "Leave it to Howard!" are more what he is used to hearing. But that's not this checkout clerk's greeting.

"You gave me too much." She pushes back the coins with the exaggerated patience that is impatience. She is polite about it, too polite, as though she is explaining to a child—or to an old man. "It's only sixteen seventy-two. See"—she points to the figure 16 on the register readout—"that's *less* than twenty dollars." She spells it all out. What is she thinking about him: "stupid," "senile," "Alzheimer's," "retarded"?

Probably just "old." He catches on quickly—his survival skills again. Here he is, hair turning gray, shopping in the middle of the morning, wearing jeans, not yet shaved for the day, and behaving oddly (those two dimes and two pennies). He knows why—he is taking it easy this morning because he has worked hard all weekend—and he needs those quarters for parking this afternoon on a business call. But she knows why, just as surely: This man is old. And old means out of it: "Be nice to him . . . he can't help it if he is confused . . . help him through it" and "Get rid of him as fast as you can. Get back to the living."

Howard seems to spend more and more energy these days proving that he is *not* confused, not slowing down. Really, that he is not aging. He relishes it more and more when people say "You haven't changed" or "You're not really in your sixties, are you?"

49

Like most white middle-class men, Howard has never before known what it was like to hit the wall of social stereotypes, to be defined by others inaccurately and spurned unfairly because of the way he looks: "dissed," in the street language Howard prides himself with keeping up on. "Ageism" is the word he reads in the magazines. He may know himself to be clever, alert, competently in charge of his doings—just those things, he has learned for sixty years, that will make him feel confidently a man. But the clear message from the clerk is, You are confused, fumbling, not quite able to cope, therefore not quite a man anymore. Instead of being a man, you're old. He has been taught, as a man, to rely for identity on just those traits that ageing threatens to strip him of. (And no longer, in Howard's culture, is there any fresh role of wise elder to replace the fading role of competent manager. Toward that end, this book will offer such roles as magi and pilgrim.)

It's worse than that. She finds another way to say, You're not a man anymore; you're old. She's actually reaching for his hand to hold it while she drops in the coins, the unkindest cut of all. Howard recognizes that she doesn't see him as any kind of sexual threat. He has been scrupulous, as he knows a sexy man like him is supposed to be, *not* to be friendly or personal, lest he be misinterpreted as harassing. He returned her "Good morning" quite perfunctorily—which she probably interpreted as the social enfeeblement of the aged. He was careful not to comment on her vividly colored nails and equally careful not to explain his need for quarters—that would be too personal. He has been careful to keep his manifest sexiness in restraint, but now here she is, not seeing any sexiness to restrain. She's reaching for his hand, just as though he were an elderly relative. What next? Will she offer to point him toward the men's room? Or take him there?

It reminds Howard of his dentist, last time he was there. Dan had his hands stuffed in Howard's mouth and his face in Howard's face and muttered something about Howard not bounding into the chair. "Have you slowed down a little?" As though anybody ever bounded into a dentist's chair! Dan sounded friendly, concerned, making conversation, but what was he talking about? Maybe Howard *was* a little stiff from playing Frisbee with his granddaughter, but that was not "slowing down." Dan was going on about "You've earned the right to take it easy." People seemed to want him to be old. Then they'd know what to do with him. It made it easier to put him in a box and set the box aside.

It reminds Howard of the dentist's assistant calling him to change the appointment—"He can't see you on Tuesday; please come in at three on Wednesday"—as though he didn't have his own schedule to keep and was just sitting around waiting for something to do.

It reminds him of the strange moment when he was waiting at the curb downtown for his wife to pick him up. He wasn't at a bus stop, but when a city bus went by, it stopped fifty feet past him and waited. He glanced at it curiously, then noticed everyone on the bus was turning to stare at him; then the driver dropped the front of the bus to "kneeling." They were waiting for him, assuming that he was too confused to hail and a board a city bus. Are people so helpful because he looks helpless, or does their helpfulness make him look helpless?

Checking out at the grocery reminds Howard of checking in at the airport recently. The counter agent leaned over to help lift his bag through and then, very patiently, explained how to get to the gate.

On that same trip, Howard returned a rental car. The agent in the lot took one look at him—same graying hair, casual clothes (another survival skill, for traveling comfortably), midday midweek check-in (a cheaper time to travel, and not when the movers and shakers of the world rush into the lot)—and began studying the finish of the car minutely, brushing the dust away, bending over closely, everything but a magnifying glass, looking for scratches. Since when did the company worry about scratches? Dents, yes, but never before scratches. But it seemed Howard looked old, and old means "incompetent" (or maybe "easy target"), so of course he must be returning a damaged car. Howard could see it all happening, just as automatically as that. And old also seemed to mean "dehumanized" or "absent" or just "out of it." The agent acted as though Howard weren't standing beside him, trying to talk about it. It shook Howard, almost disabled him, as though he *were* too old to be competent. Ordinarily—those proud survival skills again— he would have stayed smooth and cool and not felt victimized. But this move of being dismissed from the world of the cool and competent—being old—startled him into near paralysis. He hadn't felt so sidelined from his life since he was a teenager.

Standing by, unnoticed, and watching—that happens at work too, in ways he's not used to. Things get routed past him; he's not in on planning very much any more. He used to be the first one to pass out the gossip about changes; now it seems he hears it last. He's not paranoid; it's not a campaign to get him to retire. They don't even know they're doing it. They just think of him as on the way out, not the comer he has always felt himself. "Comer"—that's the irony. He has been waiting for the status that comes with seniority; now he knows what "senior" really means.

For all the jarring strangeness of people treating him as "old," it is, too, a jarringly familiar sensation, this being put under wraps, consigned to a niche, straitjacketed, involuntarily closeted, this feeling that he can't break loose and be himself. The moment you are allowed between all the time you are too young, not senior enough, and the time you are too senior must be very brief. He must have missed that moment of being there.

Howard has no problem with the signs of aging that *he* notices: minor health nuisances, odd aches and pains, folds of skin appearing here and there, the doctor wanting to monitor his prostate with semiannual PSA blood tests, maybe occasional forgetfulness, maybe even a little sexual slowdown. Such things seem normal, manageable, maybe even interesting, like moving into a new neighborhood and getting acquainted. No put-down, no stigma, no threat to identity or self-esteem. No blame or shame, just the way things are, and that's OK. He can accept himself as an aging Howard; he's still Howard. It's not the aging that bothers him, it's the new version of barricades and deflection.

Conventional wisdom might regard Howard as a victim of the typical male's addiction to achievement, power, mastery, and control, an addiction white males can indulge in middle age, before they retreat to join the rest of the human race as victims of middle-aged-white-male power. Howard has lived by getting repeated fixes of power, and when they are withheld he has painful withdrawal symptoms; so goes conventional wisdom. Such conventional wisdom is right insofar as it reminds Howard that feeling sidelined is the norm and the stabs at mastery and control are the temporary exceptions; that's a liberating correction for Howard's sensation that being fully in charge of his own life is the norm, from which he has now fallen. His "aging," in restoring him to a degree of helplessness and yearning, is restoring him to life as it really is and as it is experienced by most of his fellow human beings.

But conventional wisdom errs in disparaging his ventures at control and mastery as distorting and wrong. They are better seen as religious strategies, prompted by religious motives; maybe not very religious in effect, but religious in intent. They are a form of a man's aspirations and expectation for a fuller life. They are one way a man tries to claim the promises that elude him. For a while, and sometimes, they seem to work. The religious purist can point out, accurately, that Howard's is a false trust, the trust that he can "save" himself by his own savvy, by staying "on top of things"—by supplying himself with quarters, for example. But it seems more honest and more helpful to Howard to regard his supply of faith as half full, not half empty, to recognize the religious urgency and hope in his lunges to find himself reliably established, the haunting religious quality of his ache for destiny and his sorrow at finding it passing him by.

If he views the discomfort of aging as re-presenting a lifelong religious dilemma, Howard faces more options than the automatic counterattack he would otherwise deploy. The aging is not flaw or deterioration so much as it is grounding. Religiously viewed, there is room to recognize that his present discontent—living more consciously as "destined" rather than as "arrived"—puts him in closer touch with fundamental realities and resources than he would otherwise know. God, who is more resident in the shadows than in the glare, is discerned and approached more readily in waiting than in arrival. Later chapters will explore this discovery with Howard.

Murray:
Work Warrior

It wasn't until he was starting down the elevator with Al at the end of the day that Murray had any time to think about Sam's visit to the office that afternoon. It was pretty painful, he told Al, in a conversation that lasted into the parking lot and all the way on and off the Interstate, until Al got out at his corner.

Sam had been retired a couple of years and stopped by for a visit. But there wasn't time to talk as long as Sam wanted, and, worse, there wasn't anything to say to Sam that he wanted to hear. Sam had wanted to hear how marvelous was the inventory control system he had spent years devising. Sam was still relishing his feat. "It saves shutting everything down for a day just to take inventory, the way we used to, and the paperwork is a lot less."

"We tried to break it to him," Murray was telling Al, "that we had scrapped his whole system, now that we just read bar codes. But I guess we didn't try very hard, because he was still bragging about it to everyone he met. I hope you shoot me before I get like that."

"No way," Al protested, but Murray was serious and reflective.

"Yeah, it really can happen. It's a setup. We do everything we can to persuade top management that we're indispensable, but we mostly just persuade ourselves. I killed myself this afternoon polishing that prospectus. It's not so much I'm trying to impress the boss—it's pretty clear what promotions and raises I can and can't count on, regardless—but what keeps me at that screen is that I really think the new project isn't going to work well unless I fine-tune it, get the bugs out, get the choreography all set up in advance, so it can just flow. It's my baby, and it's up to me to set it on its feet and get it up to speed. It won't go right unless I make it happen, and if it bombs, or even if it only falters a little, it's my fault. Like that guy in the sculpture in front of the health club, carrying the world on his back, I can't drop it. There's no one else to pick it up, and it can't run by itself.

"That's why I've got to chase out after supper tonight—and I hate it—to this church committee meeting. They'll screw up if I'm not there. It's true; they really will—look what happened to the budget last year. But why do I take it so personally, make it *my* screwup?

"That's what Sam persuaded himself for forty years, Mr. Indispensable, and once you're seduced into playing God that way, you don't want to hear anything different. Especially you don't want to hear that you failed. Sam can't bear to hear that his inventory system isn't perfect. The problem isn't that someone else has taken over, or even that there's a new system; the problem is that Sam's system wasn't perfect—that's what he's afraid of—and if it isn't perfect, it failed, and if the project fails or the system fails, *you* fail. That's the nasty secret about playing Superman: It's a setup to feel like a klutz, because you're giving all your chips to be played by somebody else or a bunch of somebody elses who are sure to lose them—and there goes the ball game. You can't make winners out of losers, even if you do lay that trip on yourself and pretend you can."

Perhaps we can understand best what all this means to Murray if we say that he (and other Murrays and Sams) are working "religiously." We often say this about the kind of intensity, single-mindedness, even obsessiveness he describes; he is hooked, addicted, can't seem to let go, seems to have "given his life" to his job (to use a religious formula). There is a ritualized quality to the work that seems to take charge. There is a totality of commitment. There is the kind of drive for perfection that Murray and Sam talk about. Invoking conventional wisdom, one might suppose that the "religiousness" is that Murray and Sam are mostly needing to earn favor with the gods who rule their lives—namely, their bosses—though Murray says he does not need that. Conventional wisdom might argue that Murray and Sam are driven by competitive and rivalrous needs; they need to conquer, to climb, to control, to prevail over all others, over all odds, maybe like a holy warrior or crusader. These are all possible and partial senses of "religiousness" in Murray's work life, but not what I mean when I use the word here.

Murray's work is "religious" because he is trying to use it to make his life count for something; so is Sam. He wants to feel meaning in what he is doing by making a difference, an important difference. He needs to feel he is leaving a unique impact on the world; he is a key player in some important scheme of things, someone whose finger is on the pulse of major energies, a solver of disastrous dilemmas. He wants his work to be a calling, transcending mundane things like time clocks, office politics, and institutional foibles, the opposite of routine drudgery, the exact opposite of the workaholism into which he has slipped. Of course Murray and Sam need to work overtime, to assign themselves goals no one else assigns them, to fix things others don't regard as broken, to keep polishing what is already done well; they need to prove—to themselves—that they are in a realm beyond the routines, the opposite of going through the motions. If Murray and Sam are unrealistic in the "salvation" they expect from their work, if they exaggerate their accomplishments, if they are blind to or suppose themselves immune to the futility and drudgery that besets their work, this testifies to the intensity of their genuinely religious need, their hunger for the affirmation that their lives are fulfilling their potential, their sorrowful twofold conviction that their lives are meant for something important but that such fulfillment still eludes.

"It's like I'm carrying the ball," Murray adds, "and if we don't score it's my fault. It doesn't matter if my guys don't block for beans; I feel like I should've set up the play better. It doesn't matter if the other guys are twice as big; I feel like I should've been faster and more slippery." Such a fantasy is usually dismissed (or honored) as exaggerated ego, narcissism, competitiveness, or testosterone. Maybe it's better understood as meaning simply, It's hard to be as special as I feel I really am.

"It's like it used to be in high school geometry class. Old Mr. Corneal would let somebody fumble around at the blackboard until about ten minutes before the hour was up and then call on me, and it was my mission, whether I chose to accept it or not, to get the proof done before the bell rang. That was the unwritten deal we had, and I got off on that, pounding away with the chalk.

"I think I also had some kind of unwritten deal like that with my parents about my sister. 'Look after her' is what they would tell me when she was little. 'Don't let her get hurt; don't let her cry, don't make her cry' and that got to be a pretty big project as we both got older, 'Make everything all right for her.' Make sure she had dates, make sure she had money, everything. It's still like that. I feel like it's *my* problem if I call her up and she sounds depressed, or if she can't afford the ticket to visit our parents, or if she's having a problem with her husband—I can't hang up until she's cheered up or until we have figured out how to deal with the money or the marriage. She doesn't make me do it—in fact she says, Back off—*I* make me, or my parents did, or something. The thing is, it doesn't feel like a burden; it feels like a challenge, an opportunity I can't turn down."

Recent conventional wisdom casts Murray as an oppressor. His relentless mission to fix and to provide demeans and manipulates others by casting them as helpless pawns whose role is to provide props for his own sense of achievement and control.

But Murray is not making up his foreboding that life is precarious, often defective, or his trust that remedy is available. This is not narcissistic invention, and it is not just residue from trips laid on him by anxious teachers and parents. Life really is precarious, less than it can be. Or, to put it in terms of hope, life can be more than it is. There is some urgency about this, a calling to those with ears to hear and with the will to respond. To heed that call and aspire to pursue remedy is not to enhance or promote or guarantee self (or doesn't have to be); it is to risk self, lose self. It is precisely to surrender your chips to others, as Murray has put it, with all the dismay and apprehension Murray feels about that. Murray does sometimes go about his "religious" work with relentless urgency, which we are about to characterize as that of a crusader or a monarch. But there are ways, which Murray also seems to know, to go about work with the focused religious abandon of the magi or the pilgrim, to use other metaphors of chapters to come.

Norman:
Sex as a Religious Passion

Norman's story is one we hear more often from the woman's side. So let's hear it that way first. Pat's version goes like this.

"One thing I especially need from Norm is what I call 'nourishing,' and he's good at it. He's wonderful at nourishing. I love him to rub my back. He can stroke gently in a way that feels very tingling, very loving, or he can dig deep with his knuckles in just the right places; that feels like he's giving me all his best energy and attention and feels even more loving and caring than the stroking. Something else I need, which he is good at, is listening. I like to lie close and talk out the day, the things that have upset me or seemed unresolved, the parts of the day I really cherished. I like to hold them. I guess some people used to do bedtime prayers like that. But I just like to talk to Norm. He listens well and he seems to care, and he's right there.

"But often that's just the problem, he's too much there. He can't seem to leave it at the back rub and listening. He gets turned on and wants to finish off with sex. I really like sex, too, but not all the time; why can't touching and sharing be enough sometimes? It seems like a beast takes over the intimacy; Norm's agenda takes over mine. Why can't he just enjoy the intimacy of pillow talk instead of turning it into foreplay and having to bring it back down to just sex?"

Conventional wisdom accepts Pat's analysis, and Norman often does too. His sexual arousal is a flaw, a delinquency. He's like the bad boy in school throwing spitballs when he should be reading fine literature. Being male, he has too beastly an understanding of what intimacy is. Sex is too narrow and short-term, too mechanical and too mean, compared with the higher forms of intimacy Pat prefers. So the Normans of the world are instructed (by the new conventional wisdom) to become more "sensitive," and they try to comply. Or, accepting Pat's diagnosis as a challenge, the old conventional wisdom urges Norman to defy the accusation, to be "manly," to affirm his sensuality and not apologize for being horny.

But rather than thinking of sex as beastly or assertive, there is another perspective—the male experience of living the daily life in sorrow and expectancy, living by that transcending question *Is that all there is?* This opens the way to recognizing the religious dimensions of sexuality, its capacity to transport and transform, to ground and to exalt life. If Norman were to find this voice, he might say this:

"I know Pat likes to talk over the day, and I can do that, but it is always something of a drag, as in dragging an anchor. The day is done; let it be finished, not kept warmed over. What's done is done, for better or worse. And there is a lot of 'worse' in each day, things that don't go as well for me as I think they should. But that's just the way it is. The routines and problems of the day are interesting enough to be worth it first time around, but they're too dreary to be worth a rerun. Especially not dragged into bed with us. And especially not as the main feature. Bed—marriage, intimacy—is for something else, for getting out of the daily grind, for reminding yourselves that life is richer and better than what you've had all day.

"That's why the sex is so important. It's the one thing that is special, set apart, just for Pat and me, alone and naked, the one place you can just be yourself and not have to be something someone wants you to be. You get carried away, out of this world, out of sight, transported, transcendent. But it all happens in a way that makes you feel more yourself, not outside of yourself, more rooted, more focused, less diffuse. It's being carried away and carried back into yourself at the same time. Back to basics. It's 'sacramental,' this moment is. If you want to talk over problems, you can do that with a therapist, or at a bar, or on the phone with your best friend—and I'd like to be Pat's best friend, too, if I can. Those things are important, but they're not called sacraments, like marriage is, like I think sex is; they can't lift you out of the dreariness, out of this world, give you a taste of an other world that is also a more real world. Pat thinks I'm crudely horny, animal-like, scuttling the intimacy of conversation. Sex *is* beastly in its own way. But somehow, maybe just because it is so primitive, it's also heavenly. It takes you back to basics, to a moment that hints at ecstasy. Back to Eden, on to Eden.

"Same way with the back rubbing. That's another way of digging at the pains—just like the verbal digging. It's important and good, as far as it goes. But life is more than dealing with its pains. I'm more than my aching muscles, and there's a lot more to Pat and me than sore muscles or skin hunger, just like there's a lot more to us than all the things of the day that went right or wrong or half right. You can't let the aches and hungers set your agenda; you have to move beyond them, follow your star. Sex can provide that kind of enchantment. It's one way, a great way, a great gift, for momentarily sampling life as it must be intended: untrammeled, healed, good. That intensity, that momentary bliss of feeling wiped out—that's got to be a mystical glimpse of life beyond the aches of life. We need that. We deserve that.

"It's like after a business trip, Pat is eager to sit over a cup of tea and get caught up on our lives while we were apart; for her, this leads naturally to sex, but only after the verbal foreplay. For me, the order is reversed: Sex seems the right way to get together, to get reacquainted, to remind ourselves of who we are—uniquely special and transforming for each other, out of the ordinary; then this sets the tone of the conversational catch-up. Without Pat, life was ordinary, humdrum. Why dwell longer than necessary in that mode? Why let the mood of the daily humdrum routines set the mood for sex, when it should be the other way around? With Pat, and especially in the intensity of sexual intimacy, life is blessed; it tastes different;

everything looks and feels different. I'm not making sex an end in itself, which is what those magazine articles she reads accuse me of doing. Maybe she is making sex the end, literally putting it at the end."

Is this all there is? The pillow talk with Pat and the kneading of her flesh contain, for Norman, the promise of a fulfilling "more"—"contain" in its teasing double meaning: It restrains and confines even as it proffers.

Norman aspires to a consummation that transforms. He is expressing the male energies for *re*birth that complement the female instincts to *give* birth, to nest, to settle. Norm yearns to transform what Pat seems content to form. Pat wants to work with the "stuff" of life, to shape it, like a potter the clay, like a baker the loaf, like gestation and labor pains. She wants to knead the daily routine, just as she wants her body kneaded. From Norm's point of view, Pat wants to leave the dough or the clay as it is, unfired, therefore never bowl or bread. It seems to him like settling for what is still unsettled and unsettling, still needing refinement. It's as though God had formed a man out of the soil but neglected to breathe "into his nostrils the breath of life" (Gen. 2:7). In his sexual arousal, like all men in their expectant tumescence, Norm aspires to that life-giving transforming breath.

Rebirth requires a death of something so it can emerge in a transformed state, converted. Pat is right to prize the daily life, and Norman, in his yearning for more, is right to relinquish it. Sex, like other religious sacraments, yields its blessing in exchange for renunciation. One loses one's life as the means of finding it, surrenders the usual claims of identity and control, and opts for the power and gifts of vulnerability. For sex one disrobes in revealing nakedness, as in pilgrimage and in ceremony one dons robes of anonymity and cover-up; in both cases the point is to surrender the identity shaped by the familiar rhythms and roles and uniforms of daily routine—surrender so it can be reborn.

The religious man is responding ("aroused" may be the better word) to the profound tease—there is no better word—of daily life as he finds it. It promises so much, for those with eyes to see, and it withholds so much, for those with hearts to risk. This is the tease of cosmic proportions that generates—arouses—the classic religious passions, at once excruciating and sublime. For what else are faith, hope, and love? What else is religious devotion, than the hungry, even lustful arousal triggered by life's excruciating double message: the affirmation that life promises a wholeness—a holiness—blended with the painful confession that the promise has not yet been kept, bliss blended with heartbreak? Without the promise, there is no faith, hope, or love, just as there is no sexual arousal without the possibility. But neither is there the arousal, religious or sexual, without the withholding of consummation. The tingling tease of sexual arousal, responding to that intensely painful/pleasurable dialectic between what is promised and what is denied, is apposite metaphor—and much more than metaphor—for religious arousal. The paradoxical passions of religion, faith, hope, and love are all aroused by the dialectic: Faith is in what is *not* known; hope is for what is *not* seen; love is called for especially by one's enemies. "Tease," "grief," "sorrow," "faith," "hope" are all words for the religious dimensions of having and not having, of living in the world but not of it, living the daily life in the mood of living it on the way to a destiny beyond.

Is that all there is? Precisely in his despair, the tumescent man knows profound hope. He "waits with eager longing" (Rom. 8:19).

Part II

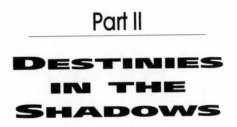

Destinies
in the
Shadows

Conscripted and Called

5

Perhaps the most widely advertised trait of modern men, and the most widely deplored, is our habit of exerting control: imposing scripts on others and imposing restraints on our own vitality. This chapter explores two motives for that habit: (1) Men are, often ruefully, obeying scripts imposed on them. (2) Men are heeding a "call"—as soldiers and priests do—to safeguard and to refine life. Such a call requires discipline.

Remote Control

One thing, it often seems, the modern American man must possess or he is not a man: the TV remote control. It is an emblem of manhood, a scepter not to be surrendered. Without the remote control in his hands a man feels as restless and testy, as displaced and unmanned, as he would feel standing aside to watch someone else pack his car trunk, or yielding the steering wheel to become a passenger in his own car, or—what sometimes seems the ultimate defeat of manhood—stopping the car to ask for directions.

The man's grip on the TV remote control—and his dis-ease without that grip—is not trivial, nor is it merely amusing and overused fodder for stand-up comics or *New Yorker* cartoons. This is an apt, revealing, and sobering icon for American manhood. The very term "remote control" portrays manhood as our culture scripts it. Remote control: the aloofness of command, not the intimacy of collaboration. Remote control: management from a detached and therefore guarded perspective, supervision warranted by super vision. If you are a man, you are in control. That's the script. That's the conventional portrait.

An airplane lurches as it approaches the airport. We might expect the boy aboard to say "Whee!" We might expect the woman to say, "I'm scared; hold my hand." And we might expect the man to launch into a meteorological lecture: "When you see clouds like that, you expect different layers of density and some turbulence when you shift from one to the other." The script calls for him to keep control: of feelings, of information, of the situation. He is to outwit all problems. He is also expected to keep control of others. He expects them to learn to react in his guarded way, and he is impatient when they react their own way. The script for males requires answers, not questions, explanations, not mystery, guardedness, not surprise. A man is constantly on duty, and duty leaves no room for the child's delight or the woman's alarm. This is the conventional portrait.

Constantly on duty, committed to his script: If the family's vacation plan—his plan, actually—is to reach a certain motel by nightfall, when night falls 50 miles short of the motel, or the family threatens to explode if confined to the car a mile longer, he drives on. When a bluff is called, when his team or his hand is losing, he raises the stakes. When it's time to abandon a project, he persists. When good advice suggests a change in strategy, it's "You don't understand." When it's time for weekend relaxation, it's "This work project just has to get done." Or the "relaxation" itself is micromanaged. This is the conventional portrait.

Sickness is never an excuse to go off duty—except at the risk of surrendering manhood. Indeed, the threat of vulnerability summons to duty. When a man is ill, the script requires him to be able to pronounce a certain diagnosis—ranging from "It's nothing" to complex medical detail—plus a thorough explanation of how it happened, plus a clear program for recovery. The script for manhood does not permit an unguarded flank: no surprises to be risked, sentry and battle strategist on duty at all times. If you visit a bedridden man who acts helpless, not in control of his own disease, you come away deploring. "He's not himself." He feels the same way, and that's a casualty men are determined to avoid at any cost, including the cost of trammeling over tenderness and wonder and the splendors of mystery and the giftedness of life. He is captured by a rigid tumescence of his own soul. This is the conventional portrait.

This popular portrait may be reasonably accurate. Most men most of the time *are* like this, obedient to the script, ever on duty. We do covet remote control over our lives and those of others. We impose scripts on and confine our relationships with others to the narrow, insistent terms of the scripts. We find ourselves scripted, adhering tightly to rigid patterns that feel not chosen but imposed. We are drafted to duty, not volunteers, controlled as much as controlling. It's an addiction we can't shake off (and there is no Controllers Anonymous chapter listed in the Yellow Pages). We can't stop pedaling the bicycle or it will fall.

But *why*? Why so addicted, why so insistent, why so possessed—or, to use a kinder word, why so committed—to exercising remote control? Why so obedient to a posture of duty? That is an intriguing and perplexing question deserving more thought than it usually gets. Conventional discussions of men limit themselves to painting and deploring this portrait of men's penchant to perform, to achieve, to compete, to subdue. They seem to regard this trait as a given male endowment, as though men were possessed by a remote control gene.

Callings

But here we see the trait in a context, as derived, not as a fixed endowment. Man's principal endowment, we propose, is something else; it is the capacity for dreaming, for intuiting the disparity between life as experienced and life as intended, for sorrowing and trusting that disparity, for praying, *Is that all there is?* It is the faith and the hope and the love in that urgent question which drives a man to control. He will do all he can to make life come true. On vacation and at work, with aging parents and with adolescent kids, while making love and while grilling hamburgers, life is at risk not to go well—as any man too well knows—and he has been led to believe that it is up to him to make sure things come out as advertised.

We men are gripped with the passion to control because we are gripped with the passion to save. Why does a man feel most himself when he is on duty and in command, micromanaging, coaching, quarterbacking, guarding, designing, maneuvering, manipulating, explaining, supervising, arranging, conducting? Because he feels most himself when he is protecting and improving, salvaging and warranting. He is the one responsible not just for making things happen but for making *good* things happen, for performing gallant rescue.

It is a calling. A man feels *called* to subdue life's sorrow and foreshortening and to enable life around him to perform to its potential. He resorts to remote control as his best effort to improve, remedy, safeguard the quality of life, to honor and wrest its promises, to make its blessings come true. To this he feels called.

"Called" as in a Military Conscription

A man is called to active duty, called to defend and save his people, called to do so by a life of sacrifice and submission to higher orders, called out from everyday life and set aside for these responsibilities. Remote control is much less a privilege to be claimed or a power to be flaunted than an obligation to be accepted, often with reluctance. We may suppose that the gander on guard duty with head alert would prefer to be munching with his flock. We may suppose that the man on TV guard duty with the remote control would actually prefer just to relax and be entertained. A man, except as he feels called to duty, would prefer to savor and share life rather than to monitor and manage it, to be taken care of rather than to take care of, to participate rather than to impose remote control, to be comfortably at home rather than in field of battle, and especially he would prefer not to convert home into a field of battle. Perhaps he would even prefer not to regard his daily work as a "calling," as he is especially taught to do. But he is called to duty, and he obeys.

"Called" as to a Religious Vocation

A man feels conscripted into a kind of priesthood, and the remote control devices he employs are his sacraments. Like any priest, he feels charged with lifting life out of its sorrow and putting it in touch with its source and its destiny, with that which transcends and beckons and affirms and heals. He feels called to save life from its sorrow and to do so by summoning the transcendent.[1]

To resume the television metaphor for a paragraph: The TV can deliver wonders but not without some expertise, strategy, and art of maneuver. Hence the priesthood of the remote control. Here is truly an awesomely "other" world—of electronic wizardry and artful imagination and close-up encounter with distant events—summoned and managed at one's fingertips as amazingly as Aladdin's genie, or the raging bull controlled by the matador's deftly fingered cape, or the Christian priest elevating wafer over chalice, or distant data banks mustered into immediate service by a few keyboard commands. It's all, literally, in a man's hands. As with the TV, so with all life's possibilities. The awesomely other world is available to enter and transform the dailiness of life, but only when properly summoned and managed. Someone has to do it and do it well. A man feels both expectant and expected. He has answered a call.

His calling imposes "remoteness." Like any priest, his calling is out of the dailiness he would transform, a setting apart from worldly routines. Like the soldier, his calling obliges a renunciation of ordinary life; the "remoteness" that disappoints others may disappoint him too, but it is an obligation of his calling. Like any priest he feels conscripted to full-time duty; he is never free of this calling, never not a priest, never not on duty.

Like any priest, he concretizes the transcendent. He must use the stuff of "this" life to make vividly present what is actually "beyond." He can work only with what he can hold in his hands, what he can control. Monitoring a daughter's dating or

---

1. In invoking the analogy of military and priesthood to characterize a man's calling, we identify, of course, two of the most unyielding bastions of male exclusiveness in our culture. Without questioning women's right of access to such vocational roles in our society, and without questioning the distinct contributions they make to enhancing those roles, we still may pause to wonder if we have identified here a clue as to why society as a whole (for it is not just the male practitioners of these roles who resist change) still often prefers males in its military and in its priesthood. The male "sorrow," the intuition that life should be safeguarded and rescued from itself, and the male calling to enact such rescue, may invest military and priestly roles with an urgency and an assurance that feels essential and may seem less evident in a female soldier or priest, however much the female may contribute other qualities and however overbearing the male's urgency and assurance may finally prove.

planning a family vacation are, for some men priests, what bread or wine or oil are for priests at an altar, the *means* of saving life.

Like any priest he risks overconcretization. He risks letting the sacraments become magic or idol by investing them with significance and finality they cannot sustain. He feels so desperately committed to his daughter's welfare that he attaches excessive importance to the only means he can contrive at the moment to achieve that welfare, the rules for her dating.

Because he cares so much, a man is caught in the excruciating dilemma of ends and means. Conventional wisdom has it that men are so enamored of the means, the machinery of life, that they lose sight of its ends. But I think the truer view is the opposite: Men become so committed to the means, so relentlessly committed, just *because* we are so committed to the ends. We want a good family photograph; we want it so much that we hound the family into posing just right, inflicting and suffering the pains of remote control in the process. We want the great vacation for the family, want it so much we supervise and manage closely the packing and the route and, once arrived, unremittingly coach everyone on how to enjoy. We want the good family photograph and vacation so desperately because we want a good family life so desperately and see it just out of reach. So we grab and hold tight to what we can reach—even when the means at hand turn out to scuttle the ends, like a soldier trying to enable peace and stability with weapons or a priest trying to grace life by regulations.

Costs of Remote Control

A man is trapped, by the very scripts and calling that make him a man, into being less than a man. The need to be in control—more accurately, the *duty* to be in control (which often becomes the still more clamorous duty not to *lose* control)—is at the center of our culture's definition of manhood. It is also at the center of the stress in a man's life and of the turbulence in his relations with others.

We can see in a man—if we want to—someone whose status and privilege are enhanced by the postures and habits of control, someone who is empowered at the expense of others. Or we can see someone who is in fact victimized, depleted, and disempowered, cheated as much as anyone by the script that requires him to play the role of the controller—and thereby denies him a fuller, more rounded portion of life. The same man who is experienced by his spouse as dominating, as monopolizing the energies of their shared life, is likely to experience himself as living in the margins, squeezed out, denied those very energies of their shared life.

Others may may feel cornered or stunted by a man's controlling ways. More deeply, they feel deprived of his warmer, more humane traits. Parents, children, his partner in lovemaking, his partner at work all know they would relish the man with his guard down, the man off duty. They grieve for this missing companion—even as they collude in his calling and reinforce the script for him to take charge.

But more urgently still, a man grieves for those missing parts of himself. Remoteness of control imposes a general and chronic sense of remoteness from life. It enhances a man's experience of being sidelined, exiled to the margins, an observer of his own life. We have said, in chapter 1, that a man's deepest dread is to have to confess on his deathbed that he has missed his own life. It is a dread nurtured from having watched his children leave home, from having vacations come to an end, from having work assignments end, from having a marriage grow old, from having community projects fade away—all with the feeling that they hadn't really begun yet for him. Something rich and whole was promised in those moments, but it has passed him by. It is lost, and he is the loser. But the still more wrenching and deeper dread is to have to acknowledge that he has lost each of these moments of his life because he has so relentlessly been on duty. A man comes to confess that it is as though his whole life has been confined to a control tower, in charge of making all flights safe but never aboard, never going anywhere himself.

This chronic sense of remoteness from one's own life is the excruciating cost that the scripts of control exact. The three-dimensional full-colored texture of life is renounced, constricted to the flat and pale contours of the exercise of control. All those traits that most obscure and distort manhood—being competitive, hierarchical, addicted to winning and to besting, withdrawn, emotionally numbed, inaccessible—derive from the duty to be in control (not the other way around, as conventional analysis would have it). We convert the opportunity to invoke blessing into an obligation. We deform the gracing of life into duty.

The scripts make men lifelong displaced persons, and we know it and ache but dare not change. For to renounce the renunciation is to renounce manhood as we know it. The male in our culture is led to believe that not only is it his place to control, it is his *only* place. If he is not the one stowing the trunk, charting the route, grilling the hamburgers, who is he? If he is not at the head of the table, is there any place at the table for him? If not the winner, then the loser. There is more vulnerability than imperiousness revealed in the grip on the remote control.

The scripts for manhood leave a man grieving because he is not living his own life. They promise to confer identity, but they abduct it. To live the scripts is not to live your own life, and that robbery leaves a devastatingly gnawing ache: "Where is the real me?" *Is that all there is?* No script is authentic, and no one knows it more keenly than the man totally committed/addicted to it. To live the scripts is to be denied the abundant life, taunted but denied. The scripts seduce, then cheat us. To live the scripts is to be forever chasing what can't be caught or controlled.

Sources of the Call

Why is this calling, this script, so compelling—so compelling that it must be accomplished at all costs, even the cost of defeating itself, even the cost of crushing others, even the cost of emptying a man of his own life? What loads it with such urgency?

There are three sources of this call, I think, three authors of the script, three enforcers of its enactment. We can call them sociological, psychological, and theological. They reflect the demands of the culture, the demands of the individual man, and the demands of the general human predicament. A man's sorrow, that sense of incompleteness and wrongness which drives his compulsive compliance with the scripts of control, has components of each: a disconnectedness from his culture and clan, a disconnectedness from the promises he has personally exchanged, and—most urgent, we shall contend here—a disconnectedness from the ground and meaning of life. Sociological, psychological, theological.

When we see a man taking charge of the remote control, or of packing the car trunk, or of the family's vacation, or of the life choices of his children or his parents, we can see—if we choose to—a man morally impaired, taking pleasure in oppressing others, needing to stunt their growth. Or we can see—if we are able—a man doing his best to be a good citizen committed to the expectations and scripts of his community (the sociological), a faithful partner struggling to redeem promises exchanged (the psychological), and an earnest priest, intent to make life come true (the theological). Instead of a man imperious, even sadistic, we can see, if we are able, a man wrestling with vulnerabilities and doubts and false starts—trying to make them yield their blessing.

Sociological Source

We men are assigned our scripts by our culture. We rescue and remedy, first of all, because it is expected of us. The culture, when times are precarious (which is always), needs to identify a savior to depend on and to blame, and men are traditionally cast in that role. As warriors, hunters, rulers, providers, problem solvers, repairers, men are the ones looked to to sustain, protect, remedy. We are led, or lured, into playing heroic knights by damsels in distress—beginning perhaps with a mother who needed her little man to make good her own sorrows.

In reading the stories of Alan and the others in chapter 4, we take completely for granted, as do they, that they are expected to rise to the occasion, take charge, take the initiative, succeed in mastering dilemmas, fix and restore and safeguard: Alan with his father, Murray at work, Norman in coming home after a business trip. Carl's wife is baffled and doesn't know how to relate to him when he seems to decline the role of being the responsible one; Howard is baffled when a checkout clerk fails to accord him that role. It is virtually all he or any other man is used to. Not greedily snatching power, as conventional wisdom has it, nearly so much as succumbing to an assignment, hobbled by narrow duty.

The culture can be ruthless in punishing as deviates those

who decline the assignment of exercising remote control. Those who challenge the role are denied manhood; it's as simple as that. They are called doves or wimps or space cadets or appeasers or queers, but not men. It's this fierceness of enforcement that accounts, in part, for the urgency that men attach to the script. "Be in control or you are nobody" is the lesson, and men, to avoid emasculation, heed it.

Psychological Source

The conventional psychological interpretation is that the control script is a compensation. A man is driven, it is said, to claim power—especially power over others—by his own impotence, driven to conquer by his own sense of being defeated, compelled to one-upmanship by his own fear of being "one-down." That analysis seems too simple, too obviously intended as a weapon. Surmising the neat flipflop of a power grab by the powerless would be a one-dimensional analysis, yielding to "power" more power than it possesses in the complex business of being human.

Let us consider the personal afflictions of sorrow and hope, incompleteness and faith, how each man, uniquely and privately, asks *Is that all there is?* Along with the sorrow shared with all, there is a sorrow that is a man's own. There is a personal destiny that is known only by its shadows. The man of sorrows as we understand him, Everyman, is in distress partly because he shares the human existential predicament that life is cast loose from its ground and its goals, alienated from itself; we will return to this in the next section, Theological Source. But the man of sorrows also has his private lament. There are promises a man has exchanged with particular people in his own life. Sometimes explicitly, even in formal ritual, more often implicitly but no less definitely, a man negotiates compacts—with parents, children, neighbors, employers, employees, spouses, fellow club members—mutual promises to enable one another's well-being, promises loaded with the best of intentions and hopes, promises fated to yield disappointment and guilt. In part, it is to assuage the guilt, mitigate the disappointment, restore the promised well-being that a man resorts to fierce control. Direct hands-on management will accomplish, a man wants to feel, what the mutual give-and-take of relationships has failed to yield. (This is the mutual give-and-take of relationships that women are longer to trust and bid men to come back to.) The more intense the initial hopes, the more intense the disappointments and guilts and hence the more intense the man's resort to direct control, to coerce the hopes to come true. This is the psychological seed of the "mustness," the drivenness.

Alan cancels everything to encounter his father still one more weekend not because he is concerned about landscaping at his father's house but because he still craves to make something come true between himself and his father, some bond of connection, some show of mutual respect and camaraderie, some love, something that should have happened long since, something that Alan has had every reason to expect but that has never happened—yet. Now time is getting short. Here is the prototypical issue with aging parents. It seems time for direct action, for forcing the caretaking and the respect: Here may be one last chance to *make* his father into a man Alan can respect and to wrest respect from him. Such an agenda of course gets encoded into more manageable and accessible issues such as landscaping (and TV remote controls), so that these surrogate issues get loaded with all the urgent passion accumulated in the lifelong struggle to make the underlying promises come true. When critical onlookers think Alan is excessive in his attempt to solve the landscaping problem, they are right, but they are wrong not to look to the underlying struggle from which this urgency is derived. Alan is hostage to the script of controlling his father's landscaping more than he is author or director of it.

Carl's impulsive purchase of the puppy has the same kind of exaggerated urgency and compulsion behind it, and probably so does Norman's seeming captivity to a script of sexuality. These are the most accessible strategies or scripts these men can devise to accomplish the bond with children or wife that they feel is properly theirs and that they so desperately want. The irony is that they crave "relationship" as much as do their wives; this is demonstrated by the urgency, a controlling urgency, attached to the scripts by which they would accomplish this relationship. It is also defeated by that same urgency and scriptedness—just as the wives protest. But that is not because the men don't *want* the relationship. It is just because they *do*.

Theological Source

Men seem gifted (and cursed) with a special sensitivity to the sorrows of the human predicament. Their expectations and disappointments and ambitious dreams and restlessnesses extend beyond particular partnerships and particular settings to embrace a general sense—a religious sense—of life as cut loose from its moorings and floundering. If women are more centripetally focused, oriented toward home and partner, a focus sometimes exaggerated as confinement, men are more centrifugal, expansive, a grandness sometimes exaggerated into grandiosity. Men are searching to make good not just promises exchanged with particular partners but also that comprehensive and saving promise that life as a whole holds, a promise so far unrealized.

Men feel called to heal and to remedy, as to a priesthood, which means they feel called to regard particular ingredients of the present life as though they were sacraments that can invoke blessing and elevate the present life to the dimensions of the transcendent. Just as the priest at the altar invests heavily in such common material as bread and wine and trusts it to sanctify, so other men, as priests, invest other ordinary stuff of this life with a special sacramental power and trust it to make complete and to transcend. Maybe such trust is lodged in an accumulation of money, or a son's skill in shooting baskets in the driveway, or a letter-writing campaign to Congress, or solving the mysteries of programming a VCR, or a modest triumph in workplace politics for Murray, or Howard's sense of what he calls "survival skills" in negotiating the mundane tasks of grocery shopping. The man can expect a large payoff. Each "success" conveys, in good Calvinistic tradition, a sense of transcendent blessing and favor, a sense of righting wrongs and restoring well-being to life as a whole, quite beyond the immediate boundaries of bank account or driveway basketball or whatever.

When a man exaggerates emotional involvement in such things, he is the priest honoring his commitment to the sacraments and the importance of their work. When his sacraments claim time or commitment from other parts of his life, he is making the renunciations priests often are called to make.

When he imposes a controlling rigidity on performing these sacraments, or when he insists on exclusively controlling them, he is following understandable priestly tradition for protecting the power of the sacraments. The priest feels himself both in the custody of holy scripts—scripture—and their custodian.

He doesn't set out to cheat himself of his own life or disempower others or thrill to his own power; that's just the way it comes out. He sets out to be faithful to his call to elevate and fulfill the life and lives given to his care.

If others experience a man as an all-controlling puppeteer, he knows that a puppeteer's lot is a frantic one, scurrying to keep voice and action going and untangled. The man is a weary Atlas, keeping the world aloft, though just barely; the vigilant sentinel on lonely lookout; the driver surrounded by huge trucks on the interstate, disaster averted only by his constant vigilance; the coach whom all hold responsible for the won-lost record and for every move on the field. The man is the Dutch boy with his finger in the dike, single-handedly holding back disaster. The man is divinity on a mountaintop, issuing thunderbolts from Olympus or regulations from Sinai, trying desperately, even lovingly, to micromanage an unruly and unruled flock into fuller life, his efforts their last chance, their only chance. So requires the script of a man, imposing burden on himself more onerous—though often mistaken for whim—than the burden his remote control imposes on others.

In Control of Control

What are men to do with scripts that so define their lives, that keep them on duty, in control? They cannot be dispensed with, in an outburst of rebellion or in a fit of compliance with replacement scripts provided by some contemporary conventional wisdom urging men to renounce their calling in favor of "vulnerability" or "sensitivity." The scripts are too entrenched; they serve too urgent a function; for all their cost, they have legitimacy. They call men to honorable duty. They must be lived with. But they cannot be lived *by*, as some other contemporary conventional wisdom urges, inviting men to reclaim conventional images like warrior. They do too much damage to a man's life—and to others—when the scripts capture and control the man, when the scripts become the ends of life rather than a means to its enhancement.

How to balance this juggling act, live with the scripts but not by them? The remainder of this book explores models and guidelines for doing just that. The goal is to explore strategies for a more authentic manhood, one that does not renounce power but uses it, uses power in response to a calling but in a modulated way that savors life abundantly and is less relentless about saving it.

How can we honor the scripts but not be captive to them? How can we make them part of our life by making them a limited part? It is easy enough to champion or to pretend a liberation from the scripts, some kind of retreat from adulthood into a primitive purity and freedom, perhaps with beads around the neck or drums in the woods or a mistress in a motel. But those are only more scripts, particularly seductive and grief-laden. Real liberation is not in repudiation of the scripts of adult manhood but in denying their sovereignty, not in pretending to live without them but in learning to live with them: as tools of life, not its master; as creatures of men, not edict of God; as choice, not addiction.

To relativize and befriend the scripts in this way, to allay the grief they cause, we need to know and befriend the more primitive and chronic sorrow that lies at the core of their power, the abiding hope/sorrow that drives us to trust and obey the scripts so blindly, so idolatrously, so addictively. We can't really understand our plight with the scripts or wrest free from their captivity until we better understand how they come to control us. What seduces a man to surrender himself to a script that is not him and not good for him? What drives us so blindly to this Faustian compact that is fated to fail us? What primordial need, unspeakable but insistent, do the scripts seem to promise (falsely) to meet? It has to do with a man's deep and gnawing hunger that he seldom feels he is living fully. Something is missing. A man is willing to make the Faustian bargain with the script, to surrender his own life, his very soul, for the script's promise that life will be complete. A man fears he is living partially, only a fraction of what is intended and promised. It hurts, he wants, because he is afflicted with the faith that there is a richer birthright intended for him—but it's missing.

This may be a wound we are born with and are fated to live with, unrepaired, and to die with. Maybe it can't be fixed. Men are supposed to be able to fix anything, conquer all, but not that haunting primordial drumbeat of hope and despair, *Is that all there is?*

As we can learn to live with that anguish/faith, we need not sell our souls to the scripts.

The Magi and the Monarch

6

The first conversation reported in the New Testament is between the wise men from the east and Herod the king, between the magi and the monarch. It is the conversation—no, the collision—that rages and gnaws in every man.

The story of the encounter occupies a mere dozen verses in the first Gospel account (Matt. 2:1–12); it is not even hinted at in the other three Gospels.[1] But the figures loom large—especially the magi—in our own storytelling through the generations, because they marshal some of the keenest aspirations and dilemmas of manhood. The story portrays the struggle a man faces between two modes of dealing with the sorrow of *Is that all there is?* and the faith that there is more: He can try to conquer it, like the monarch, or he can quest, trusting the untamed power that lures him from beyond the familiar.

1. We may find the same dialectic expressed in feminine images in Luke's birth stories. Matthew tells of the magi's defiance of traditional masculine norms (embodied by Herod) to accomplish the truer masculine destiny of connecting with the savior. Luke tells of two women on the cusp, two women who found their truer destiny in disregarding standard expectations of femininity—Elizabeth in her menopausal pregnancy and Mary in her virgin motherhood (underscored by homelessness). Matthew, for whom the traditional liturgical symbol is a man, makes his birth story a story of men: Besides the wise men and Herod, there is emphasis on the male lineage of Jesus, on Joseph's dilemmas in dealing with Mary's pregnancy and with Herod's threat, and on Joseph's coming to terms with his identity as the father who is not the father. But "manly" men only; no shepherds or angels. Mary is scarcely mentioned: just twice as Joseph's spouse and once as Jesus' mother. She is given no voice or persona of her own.

The struggle of the magi and the monarch, of course, previews the life-and-death struggle between Jesus and the worldly kingdom. As a helpless infant, Jesus was spared Herod's slaughter. As an adult man, he chose not to be spared.

Matthew's account is sparse and straightforward but is much embellished in our usual retelling. Some apparently wise men from the east (later legend calls them magi, a kind of upgraded magician, numbers them as three, and gives them names) found evidence in the stars of one newly born to be king of the Jews, and they set out to worship him. They arrived at the king's palace in Jerusalem (thereby abandoning, legend says, their trust in the star). King Herod, feeling challenged by this rival, feigned alliance with the mission of the visitors. He mimicked their trust in a mystical wisdom and their mood of worship; claiming his intention to worship too, he mustered his own council of wise men to discover where the new king was to be born. He directed the visitors to Bethlehem as his emissaries and asked for their report back. As the wise men put distance between themselves and the king, the allure of the alliance apparently faded and they came to understand him as a danger. They regained their wisdom; they regained their openness to the star and to dreams; they regained their mood of worship and of giving. They followed the star again, heeded a dream warning them against Herod, and knelt before Jesus with their gifts.

As for Herod, separated from the mitigating alliance with the wise men, he turned violently murderous—as, apparently, monarchy must eventually become—and ordered the slaughter of all boys under two in Bethlehem.[2] (Alerted by a dream, Joseph had rushed his family into refuge in Egypt.)

So goes the exchange between monarch and magi, inevitable antagonists tempted into alliance—between strong man and wise men, between entrenched lord of the palace and itinerant pilgrims from alien places, between guardian of the established order and searchers for the new, between the wily

2. This is reminiscent of the deadly infanticidal fear evidenced by Oedipus' kingly father (see chapter 3). In both cases, the death threat was foiled and transmuted into exile. It is part of Matthew's sensitivity to male-oriented issues that in his story Jesus is not born homeless—only in Luke is there the parents' long trek from Galilee to Bethlehem—but is rendered so by the monarch's rivalry, made homeless refugee first in Egypt, then in Nazareth.

and the trusting, between military power and mystical power, between science and art. It's the tumultuous exchange that goes on within each man. Steeped in sorrow and confronted with the prospect of a newborn savior, monarch and magi respond in their own ways. The monarch is scripted to control, command, capture, coerce, to exploit the new power and make it work for him; if not, it's a rival to be destroyed. The magus is scripted to search and probe and wonder and listen and kneel.

The way of the magi is glamorously enticing and fearfully risky, uncharted, dreamlike; as follower and heeder, rather than ruler, it borders sellout, loss of identity. The way of the monarch is beguilingly assuring—and loaded with catastrophic death.

Each of us aspires to be one of the magi: wise man, steadfast follower of the star, venturing courageously on the risky journey, bearer of gifts, true worshiper of the true savior, confidant to a king, and trusted envoy, flexible in mission, open and trusting yet disciplined and faithful.

And each of us dreads to be one of the magi: unwise man, impetuous wanderer from home, off course and arriving at the wrong destination, unwitting envoy of an evil king, naively complicit, in our unguarded recklessness, to a tragic slaughter of innocents.

Each of us aspires to be the monarch: commanding, summoning and sending forth, backed by huge resources of knowledge and staff, keeping his own secretive counsel, making his own firm decisions, maneuvering deftly to high stakes, manipulating powerful forces to his own ends.

And each of us dreads being trapped as Monarch: embodiment and protector of a tyrannical status quo, impotent pretender, captive and programmed, Frankenstein and Wizard of Oz, unfree to choose newness and goodness but scripted to be a tool of the established and of evil, finally slave more than sovereign.

Each of us longs for the unabashed singular authority and power of the monarch standing alone and supreme. Each of us longs for the companionship—it seems inevitable that the magi should travel in a group—that apparently belongs to adventurers and pilgrims.

The conversation between the magi and the monarch is the skirmish between the centrifugal and centripetal forces swirling in every man, sucking outward and away, maybe scattering, or inward, tighter, denser; between the venturer and the warden, missionary and pope; in the most traditional of American images, between the cowboy, who must live beyond the fences and under the stars, and the rancher, who must guard his fences and his stable. The magus in a man longs to break loose, just follow the star, compelling, however faint, into a new life, to find the real king—newborn, of course—who is worthy of the worship so far poured out on ever-deadening icons: out the door, sometimes of workplace, sometimes of church, sometimes of household, the open door that has become too beckoning, too promising, too insistent. But the monarch in a man claims him to guard the gate, protect the status quo, marshal and ally with the resources of the Establishment: to resist the intrusion of any novelty, risk, or wonder and especially to resist his own straying.

Every man, straight as often as gay, lives in a closet, protecting from scrutiny the vitalities and energies that remain unhonored and undeployed. The magus in us searches for ways to escape the closet and to mobilize into public and productive action our imagination, our sexuality, our tenderness, and our many other life secrets. The Herod in us fortifies the closet doors, lest loose energies assault and undermine established ways.

The magus—whether adolescent, midlife, retired, or somewhere in between—knows there is exciting and gratifying work to do, work that promises challenge and joy; it's calling from just around the corner, and we just have to make the effort to turn that corner. The monarch adds up the health and retirement benefits and the dependents who count on them. The magus wants to travel, literally, to places of delight and surprise; the monarch savors hot showers, and familiar language, and the need to get leaves raked and educate the children and stay near aging parents. The magus is caught up in the idealism of a political campaign to protect the environment; the monarch is reluctant to antagonize. Among the magi is the father who, albeit tremblingly, urges his daughter on to risky unsure life choices. The monarch father runs her down his checklist of job security and benefits. The magus sends her off with "Have fun," the monarch with "Be careful." As he ages, the magus welcomes the novelty and promise of each new year, something "more" to be added to the past; the monarch fears the threats of the new year, the risk of losing what has been.

With his life partner, the magus knows that whatever intimacy they enjoy is only a beginning and a promise; a star rising in the east beckons across frontiers as the magus ventures vulnerabilities and gives voice to closeted things like fear and faith and hope. But, as always, the magus is contested by a monarch whose priority is to protect what is and therefore is bound to repel and divert the risks the magi carry, like so much infection from afar: "The marriage is a good working relationship; let's not rock the boat."

It is important to recognize—as post-Matthew tradition insists—that the magi from the east knew a good deal about monarchy before they set out; we picture them finely robed, not in beggar's rags or plain pilgrim cloaks. Legend surmises that they were kings themselves. If so, we may assume that it was precisely their dissatisfaction with monarchy, a monarchical version of midlife crisis, that urged them on their pilgrimage in the first place. Yet the ambivalence cannot be left behind, this attraction to familiar monarchy along with their commitment to strange star and a new kind of king. When conventional kingship failed, they were drawn to the star. When the star faded or faltered, they were drawn to the palace in Jerusalem like a moth to the flame.[3]

Of course we want it both ways. No one wants to give up the gains of being monarch or the gains of being magus. Monarch and magus dally in alliance, in our stories as in Matthew's. But monarch and magus seem to require a choice, so mutually contradictory do they appear, in our stories as in Matthew's. Trying to have it both ways deadens the soul, because we have neither. More is less.

Journeying with the Magi

It is the magi who tug more deeply at the soul. They take the religious high road. The monarch reminds us that when we try the hardest to save our life, we lose. The magi embody the

---

3. If the reader has been swatting throughout this chapter at the image of a monarch as a butterfly, the irony of the image should be trusted as conveying the ambiguity and ambivalence that monarchy elicits for us.

daring promise that by yielding we win. The monarch, above all, is determined to stay in control. The magi, above all, seem quite ready to relinquish control; they are followers—they follow the star, they follow Herod's directions, they follow the message of the dream—abruptly changing course every time. Though the monarch wields power, though he staunchly avoids becoming passive and pliant, though he gives highest priority to maintaining his status, he loses. Though the magi yield their lives, their self-control surrendered to the mysteries of the star, to alien land, to mistaken goals, to zigzag course changes, they prevail. They find a way to be losers and followers that puts them on a heady and effective mission, honoring their call, bearing gifts, avoiding catastrophe, discovering a savior. They find a way to be followers that leads us to esteem them: Though the Bible doesn't, we call them kings.

We meet the magi as we meet ourselves, strangers already on the journey. Their origins are obscure. From somewhere out of the east, they are a mystery, even as they pursue a mystery. They are on a single-minded and grand mission—they come to worship a king—but it is not at all clear how it got started or why they are so overcommitted or exactly who the king is or where he is to be found. We know them as we know ourselves, as men called, but we cannot well identify the call. We know them as we know ourselves, as conscripted, as loyally following a script, but we no longer know its author or outcome. We know ourselves as steadfastly pursuing our goals—the ordinary daily manly goals to achieve and provide and father, which somehow seem part of grander goals, we are sure—but never are we quite sure how or why we got on this fast track. The magi—we—are locked onto a star, a guide and a goal of some puzzlement and of dubious reliability that transcends and withstands explanation.

The longing deepest in us is to travel with the magi.

But the tug of the monarch cannot be shaken off. It seems foregone, not an accident or surprise, that the magi made a rest stop at Herod's palace to beg for help. The magus teeters on the cusp of faith and fear. He is out of his depth, and it is inevitable that he flees in fear momentarily to the monarch for authority and map. He craves a jump start, a dash of worldly wisdom to ground his heavenly wisdom. The journey of the magi is noble and also reckless, alluring and appalling.

For the magi's journey, like any adventurer's odyssey, any liberator's maneuver, casts profound shadows, runs into abrupt dead ends. In leaving settled boundaries and crossing the frontier, the magi find themselves strangers, lost, lonely, blundering. As steadfast as they intend to be, perhaps even because they have so uncritically and resolutely followed their mission, they go tragically astray. They knock on the wrong door in the wrong city, find the wrong king. Worse, their blundering triggers catastrophe, the slaughter of many innocents, and almost costs the life of the very king they seek. They don't just find the wrong king, they find the evil king; they mobilize just the forces counter to those they intended.

Their story, at the beginning of the life of Jesus, recalls another story, at the outset of the life of the Hebrew people, their exodus from Egypt (which also occasioned a slaughter of innocents). In escaping another monarch, and breaking through the formidable frontier of the Red Sea, the people despaired to find themselves wandering in bleak wilderness (Exodus 16). They were ready, often, to trade away again their liberation for the comforting structures of captivity. Take us back to Egypt, they begged Moses. At least we knew our way around and were not lost strangers. If they had encountered a monarch's palace, surely it would have proved a haven that halted their journey. As it was, in their terror they constructed a monarch as best they could, the golden bull, and surrendered their faith to it (Ex. 32).

The story of the magi recalls other stories, or other fears, of our own brave and tentative ventures—with women, with work, with hobbies, with community projects, with ideas, with feelings, with parents, with children. There have been many journeys risked beyond frontiers, out of captivities, and, abruptly, into wilderness and estrangement and blundering and the very destruction of our purpose. We discover we have come close to killing just the newborn life we seek.

Magi, literally, don't know what they are doing, where they are going. That's the point and the lure of the magi option, also its excruciating anguish. With the straitjacket shed, I am stunned to find myself naked. The nakedness, we know, is prerequisite to rebirth; it is also intolerable.

We—like the magi—know more clearly that we are steadfastly on a track than that we are on the *right* track. So we do understand what it was that made the magi seek out the palace and try to find from someone in authority a ratification and new impetus for their journey. And we are drawn too by the decisive analysis and action of the monarch. It is not hard to imagine the visitors from the east being spellbound, conned, as they watched the monarch swing into action and pull the levers of power and authority. We are all easily seduced by such self-confident bluster. We, like they, can easily be recruited into the service of preserving the old king and the established kingdom.

But we—like the magi—also know, from the occasions of grace that have been vouchsafed to us, that it has been precisely in those moments in which we found ourselves renouncing monarchy and tolerating lostness that we have been surprised by fresh direction and power. It is moments—with spouse or family or work or solitude—of confessed confusion or blunder or vulnerability that have been re-deemed as moments of discovery or deepening or direction. Putting the monarch behind them, the magi were reclaimed by their star and found the new king.[4]

Modern Magi

Perhaps we can now understand Donna and Carl (chapter 4) a little more precisely. The confrontation between them can be understood as a confrontation between magus and monarch. From Carl's point of view, he trusts his intuition, his "star," to venture newborn ways like puppies and ice-cream cones; Donna, threatened by change and loss of control, fortresses herself off. Or Donna could claim the magi mantle, as one probing for meaningful depth and freshness, against Carl as repressive monarch.

But the more important confrontation between magi and monarch is the one that goes on inside of Carl. The monarch Carl most fears and resents is not the monarch he sees in Donna

---

4. The monarch within us and among us has been trying to give scrutiny to that star ever since, trying to pin it down, wrestle it to reveal a pedigree. If only three planets really *were* in confluence in 4 B.C., all would be safely rooted, scientifically explained, demystified. If only I had some scientific confirmation that the commitment I once made—to spouse, to career, to "being good," whatever, the commitment that launched my journey—was securely ordained and warranted.

but the monarch he recognizes in himself. Or perhaps it is the monarch he does *not* recognize in himself and thereby allows to surface. When Donna summons him to "responsibility," she is only rehearsing a script that Carl already feels too obligated to (and smothered by). He has been trained to occupy the throne—which shows in the insistently monarchlike way he plays magus, insistent and arbitrary about puppy and cones. He is attracted to the monarch role. When he resists Donna's plea to be "more responsible," he has to resist a little harder because he is resisting his own attraction to it. He is not just drawn to the trusting freedom of the magi but driven to it. "Liberation" becomes a new script, decidedly unliberating. "We *must* be loose," is the ironic message: monarch in magi clothing.

It is Carl's monarchy in disguise that most upsets Donna: his drivenness, his insistence. A "true" magus she might find delightful. And this drivenness is compelled by Carl's continuing unconscious struggle with the monarch script. When magi set out to follow a star, they need to find some decisive way to lay down their crowns and renounce their thrones, to leave such things freely behind them. But they can't do that until they admit they possess (or are possessed by) them. Come clean, we want to say to the wise men, are you magi just for a season, just for one pageant? Are you setting out on pilgrimage with retinues of servants and stockpiles of supplies, with a cellular phone to keep in touch with palace doings, with a stuffed Swiss bank account, with your eye on selling your story to the *Baghdad Enquirer* or developing a magi theme park? Come clean, we want to say to Carl, tell us how attracted you still are to the trappings of monarchy, its lonely power, its enforcement of agendas, the being courted and bowed to. *Then* go off on your impulse shopping or your backpack weekend or your sudden romp with the kids. Then you'll believe it more, and so will we, and enjoy it too.

Leave one behind. You can't be both magi and monarch—that's the clarifying wisdom for Carl.

And for Murray too. Perhaps the story of the magi and the monarch can give Murray some vocabulary for thinking about his own addiction to his work and to the myth of his indispensability. Murray, like most men, aspires to the journey of the magi—he says as much—to follow a star leading out of discontent into a sense of meaning and destiny and fresh life, into the realm of the newborn. That's what Murray is struggling to achieve with his workaholism. But he is trying to accomplish the gift of the magi with the script of the monarch, a script that is in the service of, and guardian of, the very establishment Murray finds so oppressive and frustrating. He knows that, but the story of the magi and the monarch may help him identify and resolve it. The futility is not just in the oppressiveness of the ways of the monarch, it is that those ways can never deliver the saving that the magi seek. In fact, their purpose is to annihilate it. Monarch is out to annihilate just the chanciness and abandon, the lostness, that is intolerable to monarch and essential to magi journey.

Confessing themselves as recovering monarchs will enable Carl and Murray to confess themselves as magi, to recall and savor and trust the moments when they did not so much conjure and impose the new life as leave themselves open to happening and surprise, to following more than leading.

Carl may recall the recent wedding anniversary when he started to plan a "surprise" for Donna but didn't. They had a custom of going out to the same restaurant every year, and he knew she liked the tradition. But he didn't; he was getting bored; he wanted something more exciting—a kind of seven-year itch about restaurants. So at first he designed a solution: He would research bed-and-breakfast inns, make reservations, and present her with the brochure wrapped in a ribbon. He was writing a script in which her part was to be adoringly grateful. But a flicker of reality crossed his fantasy; he knew she wouldn't like this part and would in fact be upset, and the argument would quickly escalate to "You don't care about our marriage anymore." That's a monarch's ways, he might have said; let's try the other. He more or less let his rising anger, as he anticipated the scene, retreat into his helplessness and hunger, and *this* is what he presented to Donna: "I'd like to do something special, but I don't know of anything you'd like to do as much as go back to Criscuolo's, so I feel stymied." ("I'm following a star but I don't know where it is leading.") It turned out she found such magi talk inviting. "That's sweet. I know you get restless at Criscuolo's; it's too informal for you. You know what? We're always talking about going camping, but it seems too much with the kids. What about trying to get a lodge in the park for the weekend and leaving the kids with Mother?" Informal, yes, but what he called "good" informal. He liked it, and so did Donna. He never would have thought of it, but she still thanks him for the great weekend.

For Murray to confess himself as recovering monarch and therefore to leave room to know himself as magus may mean for him to become less furtive about the second drawer of his desk. That's where he keeps what he calls, self-mockingly, his "sonnets." They are not, technically, sonnets. But it is poetry. The same Murray who savors and polishes words on his office computer has secret pages covered with penned words ventured and replaced and rearranged. Arrows pluck and reconnect phrases in experiments of sound. Puns abound. Everyone knows about Murray and his sonnets, but no one has ever seen them. The furtiveness is about what's on the pages, about submitting them to scrutiny (ironically, the opposite of his compulsion to blanket other desks with his office reports and memorandums). "I don't know what I'm doing," he says about his sonnets. And that mild terror is precisely what leaves room for unburdened delight, the meaning and affirmation he craves, which eludes him in his work.

When Magi Get Lost

The story of the magi leads us into an old squabble: "Why won't men stop and ask for directions?" The complaint is standard fare for cartoons, stand-up comedians, and front-seat sparring. ("Why not just ask at that gas station?" "Because I know it should be two blocks north of here and then east.") The story of the magi supplies a ready rejoinder: Look at what happened when they did stop and ask! They almost destroyed their mission; they unleashed a slaughter of innocents. They would have done better just to stay with the star and keep going.

The rejoinder is more than a quip. I take it here as making a serious point.

There appear to be two strategies for finding one's way around a strange neighborhood—more generally, how to behave when lost. Call them "radar-guided" and "gyroscope-guided" (or perhaps, in this chapter, "Herod-guided" and "star-guided"). Each mode seems to be the favorite of one of the genders. Women, more relational and more sensate (it may not be misleading to say women are more other-directed and men more self-directed), check out the surroundings as they go. ("It seems like it should be near that park." "I'm sure we passed that deli before." "Just stop and let me ask that woman.") A woman is interactive (as we say these days) with her environment. She steers herself by landmarks. She is eager to consult her environment for feedback. Men are guided more by an inner map— is it too startling to call it a form of intuition or a sense of revelation?—which they trust to point them reliably toward the outer reality, as a compass is pulled by magnetic true north— or as a wise man is drawn by a star. Something inside corresponds to, reveals, promises, propels, toward a destiny/destination not now visible, which the man trusts *is* there and *is* reachable. We are, of course, talking about more than how a man navigates in an unfamiliar part of town but rather how he navigates through life. We are talking about being lost in strange surroundings as metaphor for a man's paradoxical discontent: He knows he is lost because he knows he is destined to be somewhere else; yet he knows he is not, finally, lost because he knows he is destined to be somewhere else. He is separated from his destiny by its shadows; he is joined to his destiny by its shadows.

His trust of that destiny, and his trust of his sense of it—the wise man's intuited reliance that the star is leading him where he should go—is sometimes regarded as stubborn and reckless pride, more wise guy than wise man. Conventional wisdom judges from the perspective of the woman's radar strategy: Just check it out; ask directions; be reasonable. If a man can't follow such normal common sense, what's wrong with him? Diagnoses are readily at hand: Men are prideful, narcissistic, dominating, controlling, phobic of being dependent, too fragile to admit they need help. That's what is usually meant by "Why won't men stop and ask for directions?" Much of the time, probably, this analysis is not entirely off the mark; all these things are true to some degree of most men—most people, perhaps.

But this pathologizing—useful as such a weapon may be in the skirmish of the front seat—misses the main point. The man, in the mode of the magi—or the mode of the patriarchs (as we try to restore old meaning to that term)—is engaging in an act of faith, a faith that he has already received a revelation and a promise that he will arrive at his destiny/destination. The man following an internal map has faith that the map is leading him somewhere. The map is his connection with the outer world, a connection he knows is not easy or even sure. But it is too important to leave to chance or to strangers. It would be an act of perfidy to consult a bystander.

Conventional wisdom has it that women are more intuitive. They undoubtedly are, in their radar way, profound in their connectedness with others, with surroundings. A man is less likely to trust or even to notice the landmarks she connects with and steers by. He wants it all laid out in a map; she says, "I'll know it when I see it." That's her kind of intuition.

But the man's so-called self-direction, rather than being disparaged as narcissism or controlling, can be re-deemed as his own kind of intuition. The map he so "stubbornly" relies on is a map *of* something. He believes that what is in his head is a representation of, even a connection with, what is "out there." This is crucial, both to the man and to anyone who wants to understand him. He is engaged in *faith*. He believes in the "revelation" he has received; he is much more likely to regard the internal map, his intuition, as something given to him, not something he has achieved. He is engaged in *mysticism*. He believes in a match, a connection, an identity between something deeply in himself and something actually "there." That is, like any important religious act, he transcends the distinction between the subjective and the objective. Like any important religious act, he knows in the same perception that he is lost and that he is found. He lives destined.

When things don't go right, the woman is more likely to feel *lonely*, the man to feel *lost*. The woman feels disoriented by being cut off from her connections. Connectedness, relationship, is her mode of life and so, of course, her mode of remedy. The man feels disoriented by the inadequacy of his internal map. His internal guidance system is all he's got. When she feels something is missing, it is something "out there," an other that is missing. When he feels that something is missing, it is something inside himself. The error, the flaw, the defect is in himself—and therefore so must be the remedy. Such lostness poses a fear, fundamental, without remedy, a flaw in his being, a religious terror.

The priesthood of a man's intuition, his magi priesthood—connecting him and his with what is other, with meaning, saving, destiny/destination—is, we may dare to say, like a Protestant priesthood. It emphasizes *im*mediate—that is, unmediated—connection with final reality, destiny. All believers are equally priestly; there's no point in asking another for direction; it's just between "it" and me. Either I find it or I stay lost. We complete the analogy by surmising women more inherently "catholic" for their reliance on mediators, landmarks as sacraments, those "things" that are neither part of self nor part of final reality but connect the two. Of course it's frightening to a woman to feel abandoned without her mediators. It's frightening to the man, too, who may feel quite naked with only his intuition, only his mystical apprehension, only his star.

It can be so frightening that he panics. He consults the monarch or otherwise succumbs to a need to synthesize or bolster his intuition. In his worst moments (as when someone is badgering in the front seat) he takes it as his personal responsibility to *supply* the inner vision, the map, the intuition, to fling the star into the sky himself and guarantee it. His ego *is* put at stake, and this of course makes him defensive and belligerent. This is the easy distortion of a Protestant priesthood of all believers; it makes revelation and grace a matter of individual performance.

But in his better moments he knows this mystical intuition, this inner map, this priestly ordination, this revelation and access to his own destiny is not something required *from* him, a performance, but is a gift intended *for* him, a promise, a guarantee.

Pilgrim

7

Here is another name, another ancient name, with which to re-deem the modern man living expectant in the shadows of his destiny. He is a pilgrim.[1]

A man seems to others well settled: in his family, in his work, in his community. His days are full and rewarding. But he seems, to himself, *un*settled, discontent, off course. His days have a hollowness and a partialness (which he may often fill with bluster), and they thwart. Something gnaws at him. *Is that all there is?* Things seem not as they should be, not as complete as they should be, not as right. Life is not as promised. Life is deflected, askew. Maybe it's him, and he feels guilt. Maybe it's "them," and he feels anger. Maybe it seems more diffuse—just "the system" or "the way things are"—and he feels perplexed and out of focus. We call it sorrow. He feels confined and is haunted by the intuition that somewhere *else* there is wholeness and healing, a blessing. He is living chronically destined. What is promised and denied "here" can be found "there," somewhere beyond his immediate confines. So maybe a change is called for or maybe just vaguely dreamed of, a move of some kind, to find a new place, or new people, or new doings, or new style, or new focus, a "new me" that is the "real me," or a re-covered me, maybe a re-deemed me. He becomes expectant. In his despair is his hope.

1. With appreciation to Allen, Andrew, Andy, Chris, Clint, Dan, Fabian, Gil, Ian, Mike, Randall, Steve.

Conventional wisdom sees this as a defect: adolescent churning, or midlife restlessness, or the grief of aging, or roving rogue, or irresponsible, or narcissistic, or failure of commitment, or just evidence that men value their personal success and satisfaction more than relationships, accomplishment more than belonging. Conventional wisdom sees settledness as normal and unsettledness as flaw. For a remedy, new (feminist) conventional wisdom recommends more settledness and relationality; refurbished (masculinist) conventional wisdom recommends more traditional male heroism and sturdiness: Become a warrior or a mentor.

Here we regard the man as in the way of the pilgrim, a traditional way, a blessed way. Far from distorted, the man's vision is deep and true, in tune with traditional spiritual wisdom. The discontent is accurate understanding of life "here." Life *is* amiss, askew, not as intended, not as promised, but this same life also points to a blessing beyond itself, in some "there." This religious intuition leads some to abandon daily routines for monastery or cult or mystical trance; it leads others to live drastically only for a hereafter. For those who want to save their world more than abandon it, it leads to pilgrimage. Beyond the horizon of the familiar world, down a difficult road in a distant place, there is a blessing to be brought home.

The pilgrim wrenches free from the conventional wisdom that would make men of us by attaching us to place, both the feminist conventional wisdom that bestows manhood in settlement and the (masculinist) wisdom that bestows manhood in conquering turf. The pilgrim finds identity precisely in his *displacement*.

Afflicted with discontent—which is to say, afflicted with faith in remedy and hope for healing—the pilgrim is in religious transit, leaving behind what aspiration requires to be left behind, questing for the cure of soul that discontent augurs. The pilgrim is departed yet unarrived. He lives in expectancy.

The pilgrim's life testifies to the religious sensitivity that life, as it is, is far less abundant than it could be, that the life we know is somehow "fallen" or tainted or exiled from its promise. The pilgrim's life also testifies to the religious sensitivity that life as intended by God is far more abundant than anything we know, and that it may yet come to pass if we confront the difference and lift our vision beyond the immediate. The pilgrim refuses to settle for "now" and "as is" and lives tuned to the religious affirmation lodged in such notions as "hereafter," "conversion," "born again," "second coming," "eschatology," "exodus," "liberation," "redemption." The pilgrim believes in the rhythms of recycling.

This chapter invites men to see themselves as pilgrims, as engaged, in their daily pursuits and in life odyssey, in a bona fide quest of the most momentous and urgent and noble kind, the quest for the miracle, the healing, the blessing that will make life what it patently is not: whole and holy, meaningful, solid, complete. Men, I believe, are blessed and afflicted, *as men*, with a lust for life that becomes both an exalted and insistent discontent with the status quo and an earnest and authentic urgency to transform. This despair/hope is what propels the pilgrim on his way.

Like the medieval villager setting out for a distant shrine, or the American frontiersman probing the wilderness, or the magi tracking their star, the modern pilgrim believes the rumor, sometimes borne only by his own inner voice, that there is healing and destiny intended for him. But it is ahead, away, "out there," in a place and time remote. Life as he knows it daily is unfit, misfit, must be left behind, disclaimed. His pilgrim faith leaves him tuned to what is lurking for him in the beyond, perhaps accessed only by daydream and wait.

To women, who especially value settlement, the restless pilgrim appears as one distant and disconnected, roving, even reckless or irresponsible or childlike. They are right. The pilgrim *is* like a child in his faith that there is fuller destiny for him "out there," even though the route remains hazy, uncharted—a kind of "what I will be when I grow up" posture that sits loose to the routines and demands of immediate dailiness. The pilgrim *is* like the young boy living his future as it spreads grandly before him while his pencil or rake remains poised or unmoving. Jesus is said (Mark 10:15; Luke 18:17) to have recommended just such childlikeness as the secret to the kingdom, the pilgrim's secret. The pilgrim *is* indeed "not fully present," unsettled and unsettling, just as women protest. He is in transit, on the way, committed to an "other" life that he trusts is committed to him. For men accustomed to being judged delinquent for these traits, this book offers the badge "pilgrim," religious pilgrim.

Pilgrimage

Every year perhaps as many as a tenth of the world's humanity sets out on the sacred journey of pilgrimage, on a quest for that blessing which eludes at home but lurks in a sacred "elsewhere." The dailiness of life at home feels flawed, bears dis-ease. Distance is required, a transcendence of place that augurs a transcendence of soul. The blessing must come from afar, from beyond, for life at hand is too tainted to yield blessing of its own. It is journey that promises remedy. Life at home will be transformed by leaving home. The self will be found by becoming lost as the pilgrim leaves behind the familiar places, neighbors, routines, social status—all the marks of identity.

"Pilgrimage is born of desire and belief," one writer on pilgrimage begins. "The desire is for solution to problems of all kinds that arise within the human situation. The belief is that somewhere beyond the known world there exists a power that can make right the difficulties that appear so insoluble and intractable here and now. All one must do is journey."[2]

So Roman Catholics journey to Mary's shrines of healing and penance in Latin America and Latin Europe. Jews (and others) journey to their spiritual roots in Jerusalem. Muslims travel to Mecca, the once-in-a-lifetime goal whose very name has come to denote spiritual pinnacle. Hindus throng fervently to their festivals, millions annually, more than fifteen million to Allahabad every twelve years, to bathe in the place where sacred rivers join. Buddhists trek to stupas throughout East Asia to be close to relics of the Buddha. In the tribal cultures that girdle the earth around the equator, boys become men in lonely overnight outposts by discerning vision and mission and divinity. In still lonelier places of vigil, mystics and meditators of all traditions hone the arts of "the inner pilgrimage by which one visits sacred places within the microcosm of the mind and body."[3] All the world is in pilgrimage, all the world but the

2. Alan Morinis, ed., *Sacred Journeys: The Anthropology of Pilgrimage* (Westport, Conn.: Greenwood Press, 1992), p. 1.
3. Morinis, *Sacred Journeys*, p. 3.

corner we know well, Protestant-dominated North America and northern Europe.[4] Yet perhaps we are pilgrims too and need to know it.

Surely, these hundreds of millions of pilgrims belonging to such disparate traditions do not resemble one another—we do not mistake the Hindu plunging into the Ganges for the Roman Catholic stepping into the waters at Lourdes, or the Muslim in the throng of hajj for the African on a lonely vision quest, or any of them for one of us writing and reading this book. Yet they *do* resemble each other—and us. Pilgrimage is archetypal, a fundamental component of the human adventure: available to all of us; probably indulged in, in some form, by all of us. Before one is a Hindu or Muslim or Catholic pilgrim, one is simply pilgrim. It comes naturally to a man.

Though pilgrimage may seem marginal and exotic to many of us, something that belongs to the pages of *National Geographic* or the background setting of foreign films, in fact pilgrimage is archetypal and universal because it is a fundamental enactment of the cardinal postures and rhythms of religion. Pilgrimage gives form to religious discontent with life as lived, to religious yearning and hope for remedy and saving, and to religious faith that remedy and rescue are somehow found in postures of surrender and vulnerability. Pilgrimage acts out literally the maxim that to save one's life one must lose it. Pilgrimage is nothing if it is not the willing surrender of self—that's the point of pilgrimage—to displacement, to ruptures of just those routines that define self, to the loss of conventional community and terrain that sustain self, to the anonymity and loss of individuality that the pilgrimage imposes.[5]

4. Our tradition seems to confine pilgrimage to a long-ago era of our civic religion (Mayflower, Plymouth Rock, funny hats, and eating turkey with the Indians) or, in suppressing it, to divert pilgrimage to less focused mobility—as from suburb to suburb, job to job, marriage to marriage, church to church, from lower middle class to upper, or as in the wanderings authorized by "midlife crisis."

5. We cannot number the massive pilgrimages of the peoples of the world without honoring too the massive migrations of our times, those movements out of excruciating despair and excruciating hope by the boat people of Southeast Asia and China and the Caribbean, by the frantic nighttime scurrying across the northern border of Mexico or the southern border of Albania, or the murderous forced marches of Central Asia, Central Africa, and the Balkans. They are distinguished from conventional pilgrims

In the disregard for such traditional badges of identity that tie one to social ranks and cultural niches, on pilgrimage one tends not to be rich or poor, outcast or aristocrat, religious novice or cleric, Jew or gentile, sometimes not even male or female—the costume is so deliberately disguising of gender and class.[6] One is simply and starkly "pilgrim."

"Without regard to sect or creed we shall find a surprising harmony of custom and practice, a harmony which makes pilgrimage a truly ecumenical occupation. . . . [The] study of pilgrimage is a conversation about life, suffering, and the pursuit of ideals and salvation."[7]

"Pilgrimage is a paradigmatic and paradoxical human quest, both outward and inward, a movement toward ideals known but not achieved at home. As such, pilgrimage is an image for the search for fulfillment of *all* people, inhabiting an imperfect world."[8] Note the important final comma: *All* people *do* inhabit an imperfect world.

"Pilgrimage is a global enterprise of deep antiquity and powerful psychological appeal. It could even be argued that going on pilgrimage is, in its widest definition, one of the few universally shared human ritual practices, and that it began in the same surge of evolution that brought about humanity's

only by the heartbreaking differences that (1) whereas pilgrims quest a blessing to bring home, the migrants—like Abraham and like Moses' wandering Hebrews—must try to transfer their home to the place of blessing, a riskier and often futile undertaking; and (2) whereas religious authorities generally attempt to coopt the pilgrim, the migrants are commonly ignored. The migrations of birds and whales and butterflies last only one season: they leave for a new home and then return—the rhythm of pilgrimage. It seems to be only human migrants who are so uprooted they are plundered of a home to return to, once restored; migrants are the pilgrims who can't go home again. Chinese or Haitians bear unspeakable risk and ordeal for the whispered promises of a new life, only to find rebuff and hardship worse than the journey. East African villagers brave desert and brigands for the promise of food in the city, a promise cruelly mocked by what they find. These are immensely tragic instances of idolization of the end of the journey and the abandonment of home, idolization of a "greener pasture" beyond anything to which we are tempted.

6. For Malcolm X on his pilgrimage to Mecca, even racial distinctions were blurred, as he found himself deeming others just fellow pilgrims rather than thinking of them as white or black.

7. Richard W. Barber, *Pilgrimages* (Woodbridge, Suffolk, England: Boydell Press, 1991), p. 6.

8. Morinis, *Sacred Journeys,* pp. ix–x, emphasis added.

self-conscious awareness of the world. . . . A practice with such power to move people calls to be studied broadly in order to find its roots in common—nonparochial—human needs and desires."[9]

John Bunyan intended to be writing of Everyman when he wrote of Pilgrim, chronicling the intimate and therefore universal spiritual turmoil and quest of the human race. He hoped, so he said, "This book will make [such] a Traveller" of us all.[10]

The Mayflower Pilgrims

The pilgrims we know best are the ones who traveled on the Mayflower in 1620. The rhythms and images of these "founding fathers" are firmly lodged among the rhythms and images by which we know our own lives—as would-be founding fathers ourselves (and sometimes foundling sons). We know their history as one of those stories that has decisively shaped, even as it has been shaped by, our personal histories. We should retell it here.

The Pilgrims first appear as rambunctious malcontents in northern England in the early 1600s, sometimes dubbed Separatists, so vigorously discontent were they with conventional ways and established authority. The status quo stifled their spirits, made them feel like refugees in their own homeland. So did the taunts and jibes of their neighbors who would enforce the status quo. Like all pilgrims, their faith answered a resounding *no* to that haunting pilgrim query, *Is that all there is?* So they took to the road, to push beyond the boundaries by which conventional wisdom would impose definition and identity.

9. Eleanor Munro, *On Glory Roads: A Pilgrim's Book about Pilgrimage* (New York: Thames & Hudson, 1987), pp. xi–xii.
10. John Bunyan, *The Pilgrim's Progress*, "The Author's Apology for His Book." If that apology and its purpose can be borrowed for this book, so too perhaps can Bunyan's defense of his *method* be cited as warrant for my writing:

> But must I needs want solidness, because
> By Metaphors I speak? Were not God's Laws,
> His Gospel-Laws, in olden time held forth
> By Types, Shadows, and Metaphors?

Symbolizing convention's addiction to boundaries, by which it would rob pilgrims of their pilgrimage birthright, an English law forbade emigration without royal permission. Our Pilgrim Fathers ignored it.[11] They took to the road. To settle their souls, they dissettled (dictionaries and editors notwithstanding, there needs to be such a word, at least in writing about pilgrims) their lifestyles. While those all around put their trust in their roots, the Pilgrims turned to routes. Their journeys took them first to one place in Holland, then another. Then, pushing what must have seemed the ultimate geographic boundary—across the Atlantic—the Pilgrims surrendered the last vestiges of guarantee and control and submitted their lives to an alien vastness and power: an unknown ocean and an unknown continent. Still larger than the threat, and somehow intimately bundled with it, loomed their trusting hope for fulfillment and renewal. Pilgrims trek *through* sorrow, because that's where they find their hope embodied.

All was unsettled and unsettling, as it is with pilgrims: a faithful surrender of safety and identity for the sake of new life and blessing beyond the surrender. One of their two boats soon foundered. So they huddled on the *Mayflower*, doubly cramped and doubly hungry. They shared, as a pragmatic convenience, their voyage and resettlement with fellow travelers, dubbed "strangers," with whom they did not share religious conviction. This early modest experiment in American melting-pot diversity was a further act of pilgrimage: It represented further surrender of control and further exploration beyond those social boundaries in which they would have felt more comfortable.

They landed far north of Virginia, their intended destination and a land promising a gentler climate. But pilgrims do not depend on sure destination or require guaranteed reservations. Quite the opposite: Pilgrims look for that new life available only beyond the surrender of intentions and guarantees. So, finding themselves (literally) outside the boundaries for which their charter from old England was valid—an exile

---

11. As is ironically inevitable, these Pilgrims-destined-to-become-colonists were already laying the foundations for the barricades and boundaries *they* would soon erect around themselves. Even while they were still seeking the gift and remedy of being alien, they were soon to name others as alien and exclude them from their colony. Immigrants ever since, as soon as they were settled, have tried to limit immigration.

within an exile—they improvised authority and invented principles of government and law which they proceeded to write into the Mayflower Compact and, through it, into the structures by which most of a continent is still governed, a new world rooted in dismay.

Perhaps what most gripped the horrified imagination of each of us as schoolboys learning to voice this story as our own is the timing. The Pilgrims landed in the most unpropitious of seasons, the onset of winter. The scene conveys a sense of helplessness that is shuddering, unmanning: the fierceness of an unexpectedly hostile New England climate seemingly bent on destroying these hapless, fragile intruders, Old Man Winter demanding submission from these presumptuous and naive boys. They couldn't know then, except somehow lodged in their unconscious pilgrim wisdom, that a year hence would be occasion for a Thanksgiving.

Modern Pilgrims

In claiming the name pilgrim, men are invited to honor—instead of apologize for—the life they are already living. Our perplexed, chaotic, fitful, restless, jagged journey is not as off course as it feels; it is the journey of the pilgrim. It may not be on the track laid out for us by others, but it is our course, and it is authentic and worthy.

To re-deem men as pilgrim is not to offer rescue from unsettledness (or coaching into heroic postures or contentment and settledness), but instead to invite men to claim pilgrimage as the primary arena of life. It invites men to believe what we presume to be God's view, that sublime discontent is at the same time a sublime hope, always wistful for *more* for us and from us, a wistfulness that is at once impatient judgment and patient leading, a posture that affirms us for what we are by seeing both what we are not and what we can be.

If you are feeling a gnawing discontent with the way things are—whether or not you are of an age to label the gnawing as midlife crisis—inexplicably and irrationally discontent with the good life you have because you fantasy it even better, that is a mark of the pilgrim. If you find yourself churning, resistant to each new day just because it is not new, or somehow heavy at the completion of a day just because it is not quite complete, that is a mark of the pilgrim. If you find yourself, at least in the fantasy of daydreams, impulsively slashing at the way things are and striking out in abrupt novelty, unexpected and unexplainable, that is the style of the pilgrim. If you feel yourself engulfed, choked by what surrounds you, at work or at home, yet somehow eerily detached from just what it is that engulfs and chokes, if you feel thoroughly convinced that there is something better in store but eerily detached from it, too—you can't quite name it or reach it, not quite yet—you may be on pilgrimage. If people call you detached and disconnected or coasting or dreamer or restless, perhaps they should call you pilgrim. If people think you tyrant because you so insistently coach and manage their lives, so desperately do you want life for those you love to be the best it can be, perhaps you should think yourself pilgrim, eager—even too eager—to be in a life beyond the here and now. (Recognizing yourself on pilgrimage, it may be easier to recognize those others in transit too and to permit them their own waywardness.) If people give your remarks or manner a startled double-take or a stunned silence, as though you were coming from elsewhere, maybe you are, as a pilgrim does.

These are some of the badges of the modern male's life in pilgrimage. Though, like all pilgrims' progress, it is much maligned and misunderstood, it has, after all, meaning and integrity. We don't have to apologize for our lives.

Pilgrims, Not Heroes

We don't have to apologize to the old conventional wisdom that presses us to be more "manly" by coaching us to become fiercer warriors, sturdier heroes, steadier drummers, more regal kings, to imitate Iron John, to stoke the fire in the belly, and so on. "Pilgrim" is more authentic, more noble, more robust. Most important, it is what we already are. The pilgrim that we are lives in larger dimensions than the warrior or hero or other "manly" models, sees farther, aspires to a fuller, wholer life. Those models want to live lustfully in the here and now; the pilgrim is more lustful still, he aspires to a satisfaction that is more cosmic. They locate the problem in an external adversary and set out to conquer it; the pilgrim wants to find healing for what is wounded at the center of things. In traditional "manly" fashion, they judge us according to our performance in reaching goals; the pilgrim is more ready to trust the journey itself. He trusts himself as one en route, not to be appraised by accomplishment, especially the accomplishment of heroic deeds. While others aspire to snatch and wield magic and power, the pilgrim's discontent with what is at hand enables and requires him to rely on the power that is beyond his own snatching and wielding.

The pilgrim knows that warfare is but a rash and futile try to force abruptly the transformations that take more patience; the pilgrim-become-warrior leads to crusades; the warrior-on-pilgrimage finds mellowing and a shrine. The pilgrim knows that the famous "hero's journey" is to try to capture a holiness and a power that can be gained only by surrender. He knows the hero aspires to wield as his own the kind of power that transforms only because it is lodged beyond the life that needs transforming. The pilgrim knows you must make the journey to where the holy power is and engage it there; you cannot capture or package it and bring it back, as though it is your own; that is the fallacy of the hero's journey.

The pilgrim wants to do far more than conquer; he wants to transform, to remedy, to heal. A pilgrim wants to do more than perform magnificent rescues, plucking others from distress. A pilgrim wants to transform the distress itself, which takes a miracle, and that takes searching and waiting. He does not simply flail at the wrongness of life as he knows it. He respects the abysmal depths of the wrongness. But he also fathoms that the powers of life to right itself, though more mysterious than his own ready sword and less handy, are mightier. The pilgrim does not merely attack evil, warriorlike; he seeks and enlists the good. The pilgrim does not rely on or advertise his own power; he seeks to be empowered. The pilgrim is ready to do more than to assert himself. He is ready to practice the art of losing himself, in the wandering and anonymity and risks of his pilgrimage, in order to find and to save.

On Pilgrimage, Not AWOL

We don't have to apologize to the new conventional wisdom that diagnoses us with such labels as "disconnected," "distant," and "uncommitted." These are unfriendly labels for the traits of the pilgrim, who is, by intent, creatively alienated, resisting enmeshment with the status quo, loyal to a vision and a mission that of course seem arbitrary and outlandish to those who don't share the pilgrimage. To claim pilgrim is to disclaim the diagnosis. It is not flaw but gift—and burden—that men live "not here." It is the mode of the pilgrim to know that healing and wholeness is not "here" but is, instead, "there," ahead, transcendent. The canard that men have trouble with commitment may be better understood as "Pilgrims are constrained by transcending commitment."

Pilgrim by Intent

If we know ourselves as pilgrims, we will be better pilgrims. That is the hope of this book. Pilgrimage pursued unconsciously is too easily pilgrimage squandered. Discontent with the status quo felt vaguely but unfocused fuels a random or trivial pilgrimage, a blustering and a blaming indiscriminately: A man's restlessness builds and bursts; he senses that he must move away, but he does not know clearly from what or why. The pilgrim faith that life "must be better than this," if left vague and unconscious, leaves a man scurrying, philandering, into abrupt changes of mood, career, relationships: en route but undirected.

This book invites men to re-view themselves as pilgrims and, in so doing, to venture more consciously and robustly on pilgrim journeys. There is a pervasive restless and rootless roaming of men—a homelessness of soul—that baffles and frightens men's partners and, still more so, the men themselves. This is a vestige of men's call to pilgrimage, the remnant of pilgrimage left unconscious. Instead of attacking this random and staggering restlessness, as conventional wisdom does (too puny and inept for the old conventional wisdom, too independent and unrelational for the new), because it is *only* vestige, let us claim it because it *is* vestige and use it to know ourselves as pilgrims.

Howard:
Aborted Pilgrimage

The vocabulary of pilgrimage provides a new vocabulary for telling Howard's story—and, perhaps, new hope for resolving it.

Howard tells us he feels beleaguered by people on all sides pointing to him and saying he's old. In fact, "old" is not exactly what bothers him, but "slow," "incompetent," "helpless." In fact, more exactly what bothers him is people *not* pointing to him and saying "quick," "able," "helpful." *That* is what he is used to, what he counts on as blessing, as assurance of identity and well-being, as reminding him who he is. Howard has been on a pilgrimage, a decades-long pilgrimage, to the shrines of Quick, Able, and Helpful. But so far he has neglected to come home. He has settled down, like a colonist, at the shrines—like a Roman Catholic pilgrim camped by the waters of Lourdes for constant bathing there, mistaking means for ends, shrine for home, blessing for the life blessed. He has converted the blessings into scripts.

There was a time in adolescence when Howard brooded as he does now that his life was incomplete, destined for more than he knew, not fully a "man." And he intuited then, in company with a large band of fellow pilgrims, that remedy was at such shrines as Quick, Able, and Helpful. The shrines did give blessing, but he neglected to bring it home. He neglected to tell himself, "Being deemed quick, able, and helpful helps me know I am a man." He aborted the blessing into believing, "I *am* quick, able, and helpful." (The insidious equation—"I=able"— leaves a man like Howard vulnerable; when the predicate diminishes, so does the "I".) He has neglected to come home and get on with his life, graced by the blessing. Instead he is still living the shrine's life, the scripts of Quick, Able, and Helpful, captive to them.

There's nothing culpable or inappropriate about having gone on such a pilgrimage to such a shrine. The loss is in staying there and not coming home. The loss is in staying there and being denied other pilgrimages (to such shrines as Delight or Membership). What Howard needs is a serious ecumenical relativizing: His shrines bestow valid blessing, but they are only a few of many equally estimable ones.

Maybe there is a new shrine beckoning new pilgrimage now, one called Aging or even Old. This may have a wonderful blessing to give, if Howard can forgive it for not giving the blessings he is addicted to. When Howard can know himself as a pilgrim who has visited the Able shrine—an important difference from knowing himself as able—he may be ready to be pilgrim again, now visiting the shrine of Aging.[12]

Surely there are attractive blessings offered by aging. Being coddled, for one thing, has its allure; for another, the delights of grandparenting shed of the awesome responsibilities of parenting; or being merely amused, like an elderly and sage guru, at the fluster aging stirs in checkout clerks and others. But these are risky options; they require Howard, like most other men, to leave behind familiar and safe ways of being a man—being the responsible one, for example. They require pilgrimage—which becomes not nearly so formidable once Howard esteems and trusts his own track record as a successful pilgrim. "I'm pretty good at trying new things," he might say. "Been doing it for a long time. Maybe not enough recently." "I am a pilgrim" is a truer and more liberating recognition of who Howard is than the rehearsal of such scripts as "I am alert" or "I am not old."

Norman:
Sexuality as Pilgrimage

The language of pilgrimage can encourage Norman's understanding of sexuality as a kind of religious transport out of dailiness, a sacred arena of blessing. It *is* that. But then it also reminds him that sexuality is only a shrine, a set-aside arena of blessing, not to be confused with the totality or import of life itself. The blessing is not to be courted and hoarded for itself but is to be brought home to enamor and replenish the dailiness of a life whose meanness and murkiness sends one off on pilgrimage in the first place. Does Norman really mean it and practice it when he promises Pat, "Sex first, so there can then be good conversational intimacy"? It's easy to be so transported

---

12. Recovering a sense of self as pilgrim is more crucial, because more positive, than the more conventional "therapeutic" analysis, which would focus on the *distortion* with a question like: How did he come to get so fixated on Quick and Able, turning these blessings into scripts? Recovering a sense of self as pilgrim also seems more fundamental, more dynamic, and more usefully equipping Howard than the strategy of coaching him into maneuvering the *stages* of life, as though there is a fixed structure about moving from middle-aged activism to later-aged quiescence.

by the experience at the shrine that you delay or forget the return journey.

Norm is clear that sex can and does and should transport him and Pat into "another world" and give blessing. They both find there a refreshment and enhancement that makes them feel whole and large of soul—as long as they stay naked and entwined. What does it do for the other 23½ hours of the day? Does Norm really try to bring the blessing home?

For an example, can he name the blessing away from the shrine? Does he talk in the kitchen or in the car about the bedroom? An important part of the pilgrim's homecoming is telling stories about the journey and the shrine, making the furnishings and happenings of another world palpable in this one. Can Norm say, matter-of-factly and conversationally, "What you did with your hands last night still has me excited"? Or is it all sealed off, one realm from another?

For another example, can Norm dress Pat as lovingly as he undresses her? The transition in clothes is significant for the medieval pilgrim, both transitions: the change from work clothes to pilgrim robes, with their meaning of removal from ordinary life, and then the change back again into work clothes. While the pilgrim robes, the sexual pilgrim disrobes, with much the same meaning of removal and transport. And the disrobing is often ritualized. But what about the rerobing? Can Norm put Pat's clothes back on again, piece by piece, intimately, tenderly, maybe even excitedly, as though he wants the daily world to partake of the same thrill they found in the more explicitly sexual play?

Can Norm make a pass at Pat in the most unexpected moment, unexpected and unlikely because it's so humdrum? Can the undeniable transport of sexuality revisit and transform the home scene? Or must it be confined and contained in its shrine?

The pilgrim's blessings are meant to be enablers of his life, not its master. But it is easy to get stalled at the shrine, preoccupied with possessing or being possessed by blessings. Chapter 8 offers still more images—colonist, crusader, conquistador—to depict getting stuck at the shrine. Chapter 9—in celebrating the expectancy of living as sons—offers more encouragement not to prematurely close down the quest.

Pilgrim's Dead Ends: Crusader and Colonist

8

The pilgrim routinely becomes a crusader. Medieval pilgrimage evolved into medieval crusade. The modern pilgrim sets out not only in search of the blessing that will heal his distress but also—scarcely noticing the distinction—in conquest of the demons that cause it.

The pilgrim routinely becomes a colonist. Mayflower Pilgrims settled quickly into Plymouth Colony. Modern pilgrim no sooner identifies a blessing than he sets out to possess and exploit it, to protect and guarantee it with fortress and barricade.

We can know ourselves as pilgrims only when we know ourselves, too, as crusaders and colonists, for they become natural expressions and extensions of pilgrimage. We can know ourselves as pilgrims only when we sharply repudiate crusade and colony, for they fatally contradict pilgrimage.

We can better evaluate and remedy the abuses and excesses that are conventionally known by such labels as warrior or manager if we understand them as those outgrowths of pilgrim impulse that crusader and colonist are. When we dismiss the crusader or colonist in us as unmitigatedly macho or testosterone-laden or abusive, we are losing access to the pilgrim that is also within, though distorted and obscured. The images of pilgrim, crusader, colonist—like other images in these pages—may help us to understand men's options with more nuance.

Crusader

Nearly a millennium ago, crusading preoccupied the men of Christendom. In wave after wave, in the eleventh, twelfth, and thirteenth centuries, men of every class, homeless and noble alike, some hauling family and possessions (like pioneers into the U.S. West), most homesick for families and villages left behind, left Western Europe for Jerusalem, by grueling march or by precarious boat, on an earnestly religious quest. They were out to reclaim the Holy Land from infidel Muslims and to win heaven for themselves. They felt called by God for this mission, this holy war, and they pledged by formal vow to fulfill it. For those who stayed behind, daily life went on but never without an inner eye cast at this engulfing enterprise.

What did they accomplish? The Crusades drained energies and treasuries of both church and state and extinguished battalions of lives. They captured not an inch of the Holy Land from Muslim control but pillaged Christian bastions of eastern Europe. In 1204 the Christian Crusaders sacked Constantinople, the grandest city of Christendom. Instead of containing Islam, the Crusades provoked the Turks into extending their domain into Europe.

The Great Crusades of medieval Europe may have come to their inevitable and inglorious end, but crusading remains an active obsession among men of our own time. We too set out on avowed holy wars, to correct injustice, to reclaim turf wrongfully held by the undeserving and unworthy, to impose justice. We too see our crusade as championing the will of God—it *is* a holy war—and we expect to be blessed with heavenly reward. And we too usually find, instead, that our crusade is futile and destructive—which seldom deters us from mounting the next one.

Crusading—dealing with the distresses of life as warfare, *holy* warfare, against infidel intruders—is a state of mind. It may take public forms, as it erupted nearly a millennium ago—or again a half century ago to dominate the life of Western Europe. It erupts again in our time—in forms we call fundamentalism or racism—threatening lands as diverse as Midwest America and North Africa. The strange and the stranger, the unexpected and the troublesome, are demonized as the cause of all ills. They are to be dispatched with violence and just order restored. There is a God-given moral order, the right way to live, and the crusader is its loyal protector against disrupting and unjust intruders. Crusading is a state of mind. Long before there were Crusades, and ever since, there has been crusading.

Whether or not they sign on as Islamic fundamentalists or in Christian militia, men take on the crusading role. In private, in our work, and in our family, the crusader may be our most common role; holy war may be the way we most often treat the issues of daily life.

As crusaders we don't battle injustice just by picketing or writing outraged letters to the editor or suing in small-claims court. In fact, few of us often become that public a crusader. But we nevertheless cast much of our personal life in the same mode. Others, with their (variously appropriate and inappropriate) demands on us, are cast as intruders who require expulsion; events are cast as slights that require grudges and revenge. Life is demonized; a devil is blamed and must be conquered, often by some extraordinary and perhaps unseemly means. Whatever a man's plight or discontent, it may be blamed on losing control of some part of his life to an adversary—the boss, disease, a clamoring child, the fact of marriage. The infidels occupy the Holy Land. The crusader mobilizes to attack the trespass.

Everyone knows that men are wont to drive cars competitively. Besting the other drivers—for lead spot in the fast lane, for the shortest line at the toll booth, for the cleverest short cut not on the map, for jetting one more car through the yellow light—is what makes driving every man's competitive sport. But the conventional wisdom that terms this as merely competitiveness or aggressiveness overlooks the seething passion for justice we harbor, the sense of deserving and self-righteousness, the demonizing of the competitors, that which turns competition into crusade. It is not simply war, but holy war. It is not simply a turf battle, but a battle between right and wrong and the translation of that into a battle between me and you. It is your foolishness—this is how we think—or your discourtesy, or your aggressiveness, or some other delinquency that disqualifies you from sharing the road with me, and it is my business to make you realize it—or at least make the passengers in my car realize it. That is the role of a crusader.

In work life and family life we perhaps become a crusader

more often than anything else. With children, spouse, and aging parents, with bosses and others at work, with the systems we all work for, with the computers that miscalculate our monthly bills, with the traffic on the morning commute, with the performance of our home team, with the way our politicians respond to our needs, or our ministers, or our lawyers, with most any other of the negotiations of daily life: Our life is being intruded upon and eroded. Evil is triumphant and must be conquered. Things going off course must be realigned by the moral compass we wield. Holy war must be waged. It's a matter of right or wrong, and that makes it momentous, not casual; that requires an uncompromising urgency, the focused vow of the crusader.

The pilgrim's discontent with life readily becomes a crusade, a holy war, a battle to protect and purify our domain, to repel and subdue a demon.

Crusader as Closet Pilgrim; Pilgrim as Closet Crusader

Crusader and pilgrim are invoked here as contrasts, drastically different alternative models for manhood. And so they are. But like all important contrasts in human experience, demanding choice, they are closely akin, often hard to distinguish, distressing the choice they require. As with many major life choices, the two forks of the trail that will diverge widely seem, at the moment of choice, virtually indistinguishable.

In every pilgrim there is a potential crusader: urgent hunger and faithful calling run amok. In every crusader there is a latent pilgrim: religious discontent with the wrongness of life as it is and faith in a blessing that will remedy and renew.

Conventional wisdom finds this complicity and ambiguity a scandal. It is easier to recommend the pilgrim without the honest caution of the pilgrim's shadow side. It is easier to attack the crusader, as macho or testosterone-laden or abuser, in disregard of the valid faith and calling of which the crusader is a shadowed but not irreclaimable distortion.

Crusader and pilgrim are both men of sorrows. Both are shaped by their hunger for life to be as it should be and is not. Their sorrow is the same. It is in their response to that sorrow that they are mirror images of each other: The pilgrim lives in the sorrow; the crusader lives against it. The pilgrim is guided by his sorrow, befriends it; the crusader sets out to subdue it. The pilgrim's sorrow leaves an emptiness to be filled by a blessing; the crusader's sorrow is felt as crowdedness, an intrusion by a demon to be exorcised.

Men of sorrows both, crusader and pilgrim are energized to extraordinary action by extraordinary awareness of the amissness of life, its fundamental wrongness, its shortfall, its brokenness, its alienation from itself, its poor fit, its sinfulness. As clumsy, vulgar, or misdirected as crusader and pilgrim may be, medieval or modern, in giving their vision voice and enactment, they are animated by a sublimely religious discontent with life as it is, which is also a belief in the promise of truer life. The discontent is testimony, bitter fruit perhaps, to vision and faith. The shadows are seen because the light is bright. Disappointments are bred by lofty and persistent hopes, a narrow mundaneness and triviality by distant vision and expanded horizons.

Like all religious calling and commitment, the urgency and the ultimacy that pilgrim and crusader experience often lead to distortions that contradict the religious vision. They may brood excessively on the sorrow of the promise unkept. They may express their calling in heavy-handed and single-minded ways. Remedies feel so urgent that they are summarily—even violently—imposed, on self and on others, heedlessly and recklessly, so that the violence repudiates the vision. Crusaders have sacked Constantinople, murdered physicians for performing abortions, and battered their wives. Pilgrims have created intolerant theocracies that conjured witches to sacrifice (as at Salem), trampled one another (at Mecca), or imposed rigid rules of access to healing waters (as at Lourdes)—all out of religiously keened urgency run amok.

Both crusader and pilgrim are adventurers of the soul. Both feel remedy is imperative, and both feel called to give themselves, above all else, to the vision of abundant and whole life that judges the present life flawed and fallen and beckons beyond it. Something has to be done, and it has to be done by me. I am called to the remedy, committed to it, ready to leave home and sacrifice settled comforts and routines. Both refuse to be domesticated to those settled comforts and routines of the status quo—often to the distress of those who would make them domestic partners and who urge a commitment to the status quo that pilgrim and crusader both feel to be idolatrous. Pilgrim and crusader both intuit that settled comforts and routines are the locus of the distress, a false remedy. Their commitment is to what is meant to be.

We can only surmise how these things were held in mind by medieval men or what form they take among crusaders and pilgrims of cultures we do not know well. But it is no guess about the crusaders and pilgrims of our culture. The crusader and the pilgrim within us are manifestly men of sorrows, prompted to drastic moves by drastic yearnings, as unquenchable as they are unsatisfied. We are driven by the hope, which is also sorrow, that dreary hours at work can mean something, can get us somewhere, can make a difference; by the hope, which is also sorrow, that life does not run downhill as years advance and spill you off to the side; by the hope, which is also sorrow, for access to fairness and justice and sovereignty over those things in a man's life he should not be in thrall to others about; by the hope, which is also sorrow, for unguarded, unequivocally affectionate closeness with others; by the hope, which is also sorrow, that moves a man beyond the status quo to modes and places of renewal, to enactments of cleansing, to purging of self (if pilgrim) or (if crusader) of the labyrinths and engines of the world. *Is that all there is?* Do things have to be this way—with parents, with kids, with lover, with flabby body, with the way people look sideways at you on the bus, with that daily relentless grind at work? Crusader and pilgrim claim a resolute *no* but know that the claim can be made good only by radical doings.

Both know that the brokenness is not trivial or casual. It goes to the core. The sorrow is profound; the remedy must be radical; the call to be part of the remedy is total and life-altering. Tinkering and adjustment won't help. Nothing short of drastic change of life can bring remedy ("conversion" in the language of some religious eras): a reversal, an abandonment of the status quo, an incursion from beyond, or a journey to encounter what is outside the borders of the ordinary. It requires an intensely *personal* enactment of the drama of radical renewal. This may be the exchange of daily costume for the cloak of the pilgrim or the emblazoned tunic of the crusader or the camouflage suit of the weekend militia—all disguising old identity as they confer new—or the exchange of bounded familiar neighborhood for seemingly endless and alien trail. This may be the cleansing of disease at Lourdes, or the cleansing of infidels from Jerusalem or Washington, or the purging of private demons that have kidnapped a man's destiny.

In medieval Europe—and perhaps commonly in human history—pilgrimages evolved into crusades so smoothly that they must have usually seemed, to those on the scene, to be the same thing. Crusades were from early on called "armed pilgrimages." The crusader was still the pilgrim setting out on the journey that would define his life, on the arduous way to the distant place where God was more readily encountered than at home, heaven more readily earned, life made more solid and whole. He still kissed his family tearfully (or took them in tow), somehow convinced that this was for their good, even as it imposed hardship. He was still pilgrim—just a pilgrim who carried a weapon, maybe a bit of armor, maybe a crude insignia worked around a cross and sewed onto his tunic. He was a pilgrim who found it easy to pledge himself to military authority as well as spiritual authority, since they were often the same. He was a pilgrim who found the military mode comfortable, probably inevitable. The weapons and military posture were not to protect the pilgrimage from brigands—God was trusted for that—but to protect God from the infidels. The weapons and armor were incidental support to the spiritual quest of the pilgrim, needed simply to guarantee access to the shrines of the Holy Land after the sweep of Islam over the Near East. So went the official rationale of the popes who summoned Europe to these holy wars (though in fact there is scant evidence that Islamic authorities much impeded the access of pilgrims), and so must have thought the recruit crusader. Raw religious urgency drives both the pilgrim and the pilgrim-cum-crusader: Life is sorely imperfect, but God (and church) provide the (extraordinary) means by which he can exert remedy and claim the blessing of heaven.

And so the modern pilgrim, as casually as his medieval forebear, straps on the weapon, vows the military loyalty, targets an adversary, and turns to violence—moves that convert him smoothly into crusader. It's for God, for good, for others; it's to improve life, the crusader's and everyone's. The crusader mode is to guarantee the blessing the pilgrim seeks. So it seems natural adjunct—until the means, in the doing, belie the ends; until the efforts at guarantee undo the blessing. It is like coercing a mate's love brutally; like destroying Vietnam to save it; like protecting religious faith by torching dissenters at the stake; like enabling a benign community project with nasty political infighting. It's easy to slide from pilgrim's quest to crusader's clutching, whether the quest is for a blessing in the Holy Land or for a blessed home life, whether for a just and durable peace for all peoples or a just endurable peace of soul.

Crusader versus Pilgrim

Having insisted on the close kinship, in religious mood and intention, between pilgrim and crusader, it is now time to insist even more on the differences.

Pilgrim feels depleted, incomplete; crusader feels crowded, trespassed on.

Pilgrim is called to acquire a blessing, to be saved; crusader is called to impose a blessing, to enact a rescue.

Pilgrim locates the predicament within himself and the remedy outside; crusader locates the predicament in others and offers himself as remedy.

Pilgrim regards the alien and unfamiliar as ally and source of grace; crusader sees a demon to be dispatched.

Pilgrim would better self; crusader would batter others.

Pilgrimage is acknowledgment of need; crusade is a claim to virtue and power.

Pilgrim is guided by his sorrow; crusader craves to vanquish it.

Pilgrim is moved by the sorrow of what he wants; crusader by the sorrow of what he fears.

In common theological terms, pilgrim assumes grace; crusader lives by law and the merit of his own good deeds and the pursuit, above all, of justice.

Pilgrim acts in penance, crusader in vengeance and denial.

Pilgrim's trust is sufficient to permit him to go it alone, if necessary; crusaders appear in packs.

Pilgrim is able to wear humble robes; crusader wears armor.

Pilgrim "loses self" by surrendering badges of identity to a kind of anonymity and a dissolution of social status; crusader "loses self" by surrendering to authority and a hierarchical military system that exaggerates differences of status.

For pilgrim the *way* is important, the manner of getting there; the means are part of the ends. For crusader the end is all; he is able to rape and plunder in order to cleanse and save.

Pilgrimage comes to a completion, and life—now blessed—moves on. Crusade, because it is so inflated, overextended, assumes a cancerous life of its own, demanding escalating investment to warrant and defend the investment already made: It's having to live a lie, like sending in more marines just to protect the first failed contingent; like renewing the bickering, with spouse or father or teenage son, because the previous bickering wasn't "won."

Precisely because (as man of sorrows) he knows his life to be lacking, the pilgrim goes through the day—or conversation, or career, or marriage—open to a blessing, counting, at the end, gifts beyond expectation. Precisely because (as man of sorrows) he knows his life to be lacking, the crusader goes through each moment of life strategizing battles and counting, at the end, conquest or defeat. The pilgrim expects life to become abundantly more—more than he can know or control or even foresee. It becomes abundant precisely because—as in donning the humility and anonymity of the pilgrimage cloak—he yields claims to control; he discovers things righted. The crusader perceives life at risk, in peril of becoming lessened or confined if he is not vigilant; its security against threat and scarcity depends entirely on his wits, his control and foresight. It becomes secure precisely because—in donning the weapons and strategy of crusade—he claims to be able to control and master, to *make* things right.

Two Crusaders/Pilgrims

As a crusader, Alan has never yet won a skirmish with his father, going all the way back to earliest boyhood. So every encounter, including this new encounter over landscaping, becomes a new skirmish, a last-ditch chance to win; this overbearing undeserving despot, who constantly prevails though wrong, must finally be stopped. As a pilgrim, Alan is more aware of his own hunger and wanting: I'll make the journey because this may be the time for a breakthrough between us, when we can finally work at something *together*.

As a crusader, Howard, feeling under attack from the checkout clerk, counterattacks, goes for the kill: "Just punch in the numbers. Your computer will explain it to you, if you can't figure it out." Or he starts composing a damning letter to the manager; this infidel who displaces him from managing his own life must be displaced in turn. As a pilgrim, Howard feels the encounter more as an enlargement of his life than as a constriction. Her way, after all, is the easy way, the usual way: Pay a $16.72 bill by flipping out a $20 bill. His habit of instantly calculating and fine-tuning what he hands out—to get the change he wants—does make work for everybody. "Survival skills," he calls it. But surviving is hardly at stake; it's more of a game, a challenge. And it's a test he doesn't need. To be honest, there is a sigh of relief when he thinks of just handing over a $20 bill and sparing himself the mental gymnastics. Is this what might be meant by speaking of "aging as pilgrimage," finding an unexpected blessing at an unlikely shrine, for one who is willing to think like a pilgrim when the terrain is unfamiliar?

Howard recalls an episode the evening before. He was taking a phone message for his wife, but the conversation was going badly and becoming irksome for both parties. "Did you say Johnson?" "I said, Don's son." "Ron who?" And so on. It was a painful and decidedly unintended and unamusing Abbott and Costello routine, but it was also miniature metaphor for so much human impasse and discontent—when a task is frustrated, competence challenged, a relationship disrupted. Howard had the impulse to shoot from the hip like a crusader: The caller would become an alien intruder, an adversary ruining things, to be corrected or purged. Can't you speak louder? You should call back when my wife is here. You are wrong, but I will make it/you/myself right. Of course, crusader's attack would provoke defensive counterattack. Holy scuffle, if not Holy War. Male testosterone, some like to say. Male deviltry, say others, on their own crusade. Just a crusader, I would say, a well-coached role.

But Howard rallied and opened himself, like a pilgrim, to freshness and surprise. As he reported to his wife later, "You know, my new hearing aid works fine, except it's in my right ear, and I'm used to holding the phone to the left."

Colonist

Just as medieval pilgrimage became crusade, Mayflower Pilgrims became colonists. The transformation is apparently as inevitable as it is devastating to the quality of life that is pilgrimage.

They didn't notice the contradiction, and seldom do we. Colonizing, like crusading, comes to seem a natural and inevitable extension of pilgrimage: You go out in search of blessing, and when you think you may have found it you lock it in. You claim the turf, tether and enshrine the Spirit, and erect fortress walls, sometimes of stone, sometimes of creed. You define the stranger, anyone who has not shared your particular blessing, as adversary and threat, as Plymouth Colony sometimes treated even their near neighbors in the Massachusetts Bay Colony. You defend the structure as fervidly as though it were custodian of the blessing, not its contradiction.

Shrines always tempt the pilgrim to take up residence. Shrines tempt the pilgrim to house the blessing, to domesticate it, to regulate it, to possess it. It is for the best of motives that the pilgrim wants to preserve and guarantee the blessing he has sought so urgently. He wants to be able to command a rerun. He wants to share it at will with those he chooses. He wants easy access. He wants to be assured of a kind of quality control: pure blessing, free of contaminants. So the shrines of the pilgrims acquire social structure, architectural structure, and history—and thereby risk losing their blessing.

For the blessing is denied when it replaces the life blessed, when the place of blessing becomes pilgrim's home. Means smother ends. The pilgrim seeks blessing as adjunct to his life. The colonist lets his life become adjunct to the blessing. In getting confused as to which—living or working—is end and which is means, workaholic Murray has built and taken up lodging at the shrine and finds it incomplete residence; pilgrimage-become-colony is less sustaining than the home, which still awaits blessing.

But ends can also smother means: Blessing is also denied when structures of home are reproduced at the shrine and imposed on the blessing. As they became colonists, the Mayflower Pilgrims reproduced in their new land the same insufferable structures of religious intolerance that had sent them forth.

Pilgrims seeking relief from ecclesiastical structures find them transplanted to the shrine, as, for example, the experience of healing at Lourdes is totally managed by the same ecclesiasts as at home. Norman finds that, though sexuality may partake of valid moments of pilgrimage and blessing, they become obscured when the sexuality becomes one more thing "to work on" in the relationship.

Colonist as Closet Pilgrim

Pilgrim seldom notices the transition from pilgrimage to colony and so seldom notices that the postures of claiming and defending and guaranteeing, which are intended to ratify the pilgrimage and protect the blessing, in fact undo the pilgrimage and deny the very nature of blessing.

Conventional wisdom also often has trouble noticing the transition and the difference. Hence it has trouble noticing and commending pilgrim. Pilgrim is easily forgotten when he becomes crusader or colonist.

In the older, masculine conventional wisdom, crusade and colony are taken as norm. Insofar as pilgrim is recognized, he is taken as adjunct: pilgrimage seen as a stage on the way to mounting a crusade or establishing a colony. The man energetically enforcing his notions of marriage and parenting, locked into a career trajectory, or damning dissenters from his political or religious or economic faith—such a man needs desperately to feel that he has arrived and to forget what it was once like to be on the way, hungering for home, for the right work, for a clear faith. "Adolescent daydreaming, I'm glad I got through that," he is more likely to think, out of touch with the pilgrim still within. A pilgrim in colonist's clothing.

There is also the newer conventional wisdom, the one more often voiced by women, which overlooks pilgrimage because they are themselves in such an ambivalent struggle with the colonizer, repudiating his distortions, destructiveness, and exploitation but also attracted to his settledness. This preoccupation with the pros and cons of the colonist leaves one out of touch with the pilgrim hunger that is still within, giving fuel to the colonizing and to the critique of colonizing. The colonist (or crusader) is neither demon or hero. He is pilgrim at a dead end.

Conquistador

Our American lore provides us with another image of pilgrimage foreshortened. The conquistador is a cross between crusader and colonist. Like crusader he conquers, but to exploit, not exorcise. Like colonist he structures his life around the scene of completed pilgrimage, but he doesn't construct shrine or settlement. Like true pilgrim he takes his discovery home, but it is a blessing subjugated and controlled, not a blessing honored and redeeming.

The heroic feats of Columbus in 1492, which we all learned in school to celebrate and take as a model, proved agonizingly difficult in 1992 for a more mature nation to honor. The five hundredth anniversary became a time of division, confusion, and ambiguity, reflecting and deepening American manhood's confusion and ambiguity about such heroics. Columbus became revealed as a self-contradictory hero, at once discoverer and spoiler, a more realistic if less noble prototype for American manhood—like the heroes of the Wild West, of professional sports, of Wall Street, at once accomplishers and spoilers. Columbus, the pilgrim adventurer with dogged faith in his vision of a new world beyond the horizons, got all mixed up in national consciousness, as in his own, with the exploiter and abuser of that new world. We had to remind ourselves that the voyages of discovery became just the opposite of discovery. Columbus was also the first conquistador. The explorer possessed tried to possess.

"Discovery" is a pilgrim word. It suggests an opening to the unknown, or the newly known, a readiness to credit, to honor, to learn from it. What is discovered is autonomous, is authority, has a right to make claims on me. Whether a continent or a planet or a gene or a species, whether a new marriage or a new baby, whether a new job or a new vacation spot or a new retirement, whether a new health workout regime or a new illness, it has a life and power and agenda of its own that, far from being dependent on the discoverer, has the capacity to enrich and bless his life. The discoverer wants to fathom its agenda.

Instead of pursuing such discovery—opening himself and his culture to the newly known, trying to fathom its agenda—this first conquistador set out to possess it, to impose his agenda on it, to claim its turf and wealth, to subdue its people.

Without needing to sail an uncharted ocean in fragile sloops—though it may often feel like that—every man knows what it is like to be both discoverer and conquistador. The discoverer and the conquistador are mirror opposites of each other, differing to the core as to how they perceive themselves and the worlds they encounter. Yet the discoverer and the conquistador are so similar that it proves anguishingly easy, for every man as easily as for Columbus, to slip from one to the other.

The discoverer wants to expand his life; the conquistador, as *his* way of enhancing his life, needs to constrict the life of his discovery. The discoverer is able to recognize that his own life is wanting, incomplete, or flawed. He perceives his life as offering questions. The discoverer has faith that life as a whole—as he gradually uncovers it—affords answers, is bent on remedy, is ally. God, and God's creation, is on his side.

The conquistador feels consciously that his life *has* the answers, that any acquired newness needs only to be assimilated. Perhaps this has much to do with an unconscious fear of what is set loose by the discovery, a fear that this alien life is not blessing or ally but threat, a power against which he feels fragile, feeble, or illegitimate. God, and God's creation, is sitting in condemnation, not blessing. If so, the conquistador is ready for pilgrimage. It may be close at hand, like Columbus in a new world and not knowing it, if he will but look afresh at the scene around him and, releasing control, venture to trust it.

The Manhood
of Living as a Son

9

A full term of sonship is the right of every male, son to a father—genuine sonship, not apprenticeship for fatherhood, not a junior manhood, most urgently not a pretend manhood.[1] A male needs this time of living in expectancy and hope, a term of unsettledness, not in command, not desperately responsible, a time of feeling lessened about himself and a time of feeling awed by the "moreness" and grandeur of the other who is his father—and his own destiny, eventually. A man needs this term of wholehearted sonship so he can comfortably move beyond it into an adult manhood that is wholehearted, into unmitigated fatherhood. But a man also needs this term of sonship so he can move into a fatherhood that embraces sonship, not repudiates it, so he can acquire the modes of expectancy and self-lessening that he will need all his life to complement the patriarchal modes of accomplishment and command.

Deprived of his term of sonship, a boy may be too handicapped ever to become a man, never more than the pretend manhood he had inflicted on him when he should have been permitted and required to be a son. A pretend manhood can last for a lifetime, outwardly strutting through charades and inwardly wondering, Will they find me out?

To know oneself securely and genuinely as son, as boy, is necessary prelude to knowing oneself securely and genuinely as

1. I am indebted to Sanford Schreiber, M.D., without whom this chapter could not have been ventured, and who would have written it much differently.

father, as adult man. Boyhood displaced by a premature manhood arouses a sense of inauthenticity that clings to all later claims of manhood. Boyhood savored and honored endows a sense of authenticity and identity that attaches to the manhood that follows.

To be a son is a fully honorable way of being male—fully male though not in charge, sexually vigorous potentially but not here and now, potentially performing mighty deeds but not yet, aware of the capacity to nurture but for now aware of it by being nurtured, potentially a father but for now son. Sonship is not a junior fatherhood, not a shadow fatherhood. It is an important form of maleness in its own right, to be esteemed and savored, in early years and throughout life, not hurried past.

The son lives by potential, by expectancy, by call. As father he will live by accomplishment, by status achieved, by tasks completed. But as son, he lives a life not-yet but to-be, a promise and a hope that is also a hunger and a yearning, a kind of chronic shadow of his destiny. There is sorrow in the form of "not yet" that is as wrenching as the more familiar grief of "no more." To appease the hunger, to assuage this sorrow with settled accomplishment or even designs for accomplishment, is to foreshorten sonship and truncate the potential for adulthood.

For the son, life now is affirmed for itself and also as an earnest, a promise of a life hereafter. The son lives in acute awareness of a more-ness to life—just because he lives in acute awareness of his own less-ness. There is time stretching beyond his own time, in both directions. There are boundaries that define his space and also make clear that there is space beyond, streets not to be crossed, doors not to be opened, movies not to be seen, words not to be uttered, questions not to be asked, feelings not to be ventured. Not yet. There are secrets and mysteries that are known and understood by others, but not by him, not yet. There are physical skills and strengths well beyond his own, but they will become his. The son is not preferred by the one he prefers, not if he is required and permitted to be the son: His mother is in love with another, who precedes. But so long as that is clear, it can be equally clear that the son's turn will come, following the father, as long as he is not trying to displace him.

It is his father who seems prime gatekeeper of these boundaries and possessor of the more that is beyond. If fully son, not lured or permitted to become imitation father, illicit father, competitive father, all this more-ness (even in the form of his own less-ness) is experienced as graceful blessing and promise, an abundance in store, an inheritance, a covenant. His own less-ness is not only the hunger, yearning, sorrow which it is; his own less-ness is also promise and covenant. The difference between father and son is not just accepted, it is welcomed, because that difference is precisely the evidence that the son has more in store. This is the blessing of sonhood that can grace a man's lifetime, never quite surrendering the savor of the mystery, the beyondness, the otherness of what life affords him, never quite denying his lifelong sonship.

The son savors transition as a way of life. As father, life will be defined by particular stages; transitions will be background, time-outs interrupting the action. But for the son, the transition *is* the action.

The son is in a state of renunciation. If he lives in appreciation, not fear, of the more that is opposite him, he also lives in appreciation, not fear, of his own "less-ness." He is not what he is to be. This not-ness is to be affirmed and honored: That is the blessing conferred on sonship, and the blessing conferred by sonship on the man who is emerging from it. It is OK not yet to be what you are intended to be. This is the blessing, the faith that so devastatingly promises to subvert patriarchal obsession with achievement.

This is genuine renunciation. It dismays and perplexes not to be as big or as strong or as esteemed or as privileged or as authoritative—as manly—as the son sees modeled in his father, as manly as he feels himself called to be. Yet all this not-ness, this (involuntary) abstinence from his birthright, this literal self-surrender, is affirmed. For the son it is the way of life (not a way of death, which is the way such renunciation will be experienced by the adult man who has been denied his term of sonship).

Sonship denied—at early ages or later—will still find its way, but in distorted forms—as any son neglected reacts rebelliously. What should be positive expectancy for the future erupts instead as hostile alienation from the present. Measured respect for the father erodes instead as incapacitating anger and fear. Realistic awareness of not being boss emerges instead as perpetual undue deference and as avoidance of accepting up-front responsibility. Honest ambition is subverted in favor of sonlike behind-the-scenes scurrying and maneuvering.

Sonship savored becomes sonship preserved. An adult man is incomplete, off balance, one-sided, distorted, unless he stays connected with the boyish part, the son he was and is. Such a patriarch (all father, no son) tries too hard, works too hard, frets too much, commands too much, judges himself (and others) too cruelly. By denying or ignoring his own sonship he denies himself the balancing perspective of hope and expectancy, the comforts of accepting nurture and care, the liberation from the numbness of striving to be number one and trying to carry the world on his shoulders. Boyhood savored and honored lives on as a hearty and refreshing component of the adult man, a powerful source of hope and venturesomeness, the trust in what is potential though not yet achieved, the expectancy that makes manhood complete. Preserving the son within allows a man to remain expectant father.

Jesus the Son

It is as Son that Jesus is best known to us. It is as Son that he lived his life and saved ours. It is as Son that he unleashed unique redemptive energies into the world. "Son of Man" and "Son of God" were the curious titles he acknowledged, this teacher whose most vivid parables gave new redemptive meaning to the son's lot, whose life from beginning to end was highlighted in biblical narrative as son, from manger to obedient death. Knowing Jesus as Son is essential to knowing him also as the man of sorrows, and therefore as savior.

Jesus is claimed Son by the opening heavens at the time of baptism, the time of beginnings—"You are my Son, the Beloved; with you I am well pleased" (Luke 3:22b). The Son of God's message is about the urgency of living life in the vitality of not-yet, in the hope and the hunger—yes, in the sweet nourishing sorrow—that fulfillment is to come.[2]

Jesus' affirmation of sonship, his and ours, is all the more

---

2. Even before baptism, the New Testament stories insist on Jesus' Sonship. Is there not even an emphasis on Jesus' Sonship in the very enigma that the tradition poses about his siring? Joseph, Gabriel, and the Holy Spirit all play siring roles. Jesus is multiply sonned, yet not fathered. A son without a father is all the more distinctly a son.

remarkable for being part of a biblical record that does not, on the whole, exalt sons. The most vivid accounts of sons before Jesus include the quarrels of Cain and Abel (Gen. 4), Jacob and Esau (Gen. 25ff), Joseph and his brothers (Gen. 37), and Absalom and Amnon (2 Sam. 13:29); they include Ishmael exiled to the desert by his father (Gen. 21) and Isaac put to the knife by the same father (Gen. 22), Jacob grossly deceived by his father-in-law (Gen. 29), David dodging the spear of Saul his mentor (1 Sam. 18:11), the arbitrary decimation of Job's family (Job 1), and two mass slaughters of innocent sons, in Egypt (Ex. 12:29) and in Judea (Matt. 2:16).

God the Son

When the early church fathers labored for centuries to formulate their understanding of the nature of Godhood, it was Jesus' distinctive role as Son that they struggled most to preserve. They needed to be able to speak of "God the Son" as readily as "God the Father." But how could Jesus be fully God, yet son to a father God? That was not easy to answer, not any easier than for any son needing to define both separateness and connection with his father, to find intimate bond without merging, disentanglement without disconnection. But they were clear about what was at stake: Jesus had an identity as Son that it was essential to affirm as both distinct and divine. Distinct: The Son (like all sons) was at risk of being merged into his father's identity, but that must not be allowed, they intuited, lest important and unique saving power be lost. And divine: Jesus was no less divine for being Son.

This stunning affirmation—God the Son—daringly stills every man's disquiet, the supposition that sonship is a second-class way of being God or man, the supposition that this deficiency can be remedied only by presuming and pretending fatherhood. The early church fathers—every man should have such a father—insisted on an amazing affirmation of Jesus' Sonship, an affirmation that may convey, as Jesus conveys a new manhood, an affirmation of every man's sonship.

The Patristics may seem an unlikely resource for the liberation of sonship. But it is as though the early church fathers, by insisting on Sonship as distinctive and divine, intuited the need to balance their own excessive one-sided fatherhood (especially their emphasis on hierarchy and control, and especially their denial to themselves, through celibacy, of sons of their own), which earned them their name.

The Christian hope in a grander, more abundant life that is promised but still known more in expectancy than in palpable presence—that hope is most authentically conveyed by the figure of the Son.

For a Savior to enter into human experience so conspicuously, as Son, is to partake of and redeem what may be the crucial enigma that most hobbles a man. It is to touch the core of the most perplexing mysteries of every man's experience: How to be a man as a son. How to include sonship as part of one's identity. How to experience sonship as an affirmative, affirmed, even saving dimension of life.

Jesus' Sonship lends contour and substance to all the other enigmatic and ambiguous images that attach to his saving power: the "unmanly" images of marginalization, persecution, abandonment, exile, emptying of self, and voluntary death. All these facets of Jesus' career are re-deemed as facets of his Sonship.

Jesus as Son and Savior;
Adam as Father and Sinner

Christian tradition pairs Adam and Jesus: Adam the progenitor, the father of all, and Jesus the Son, the savior of all. Adam is emblem of the problem, and Jesus the Christ, the new Adam, is emblem of the solution; Adam brings sin into the world and Christ brings saving. Nothing is more central to traditional Christian understanding than that formula. Does it get at least part of its power and meaning from the dialectic between immoderate fatherhood and prodigious sonhood? Does Adam's sinfulness have something to do with being unmitigated father? Does Jesus' power to make healthy and whole have something to do with exercising sonship in an exaggerated or total or particularly genuine way, compensating for Adam's one-sided patriarchy?

After all, Adam is exclusively father, father to all, untempered by any term of sonship. Son is exactly what he never was, the only man who was never a son. In corrective balance, Jesus is unremittingly portrayed, by creed and by narrative, as son. Fatherhood is one dimension of experience denied to Jesus; he is portrayed without hints of a sexuality that would make him father, resolutely separated from fatherhood in the Godhead and from any earthly father, the only man never conventionally fathered.

Adam is "only" father, never son; Jesus is "only" son and never father. That contrast is clear. So is the understanding of Adam as agent for sin, Jesus as agent for saving. Is there a connection? Is it Adam's fatherhood, unmitigated by sonship, that is occasion for his decisive distortion of the human or male condition? Is there something particularly remedial and restorative about Jesus' answering that sin with unmitigated sonship?

Does Adam help us better to see how it is for us that life is radically distorted and distorting when we deny sonship and pose as all-father?

If it *is* denial of sonship that distorts and restoration of sonship that saves, this may recommend a similar dialectic within each man. Can each of us find in rediscovery and reaffirmation of sonship—even if that *feels* like a wrenching renunciation of the familiar postures of "fatherhood"—a needed and holy healing for the distortions of an overweening patriarchal existence?[3]

---

3. The more traditional interpretations of Adam as sinner and Jesus as savior usually focus on sexuality or on presumption and disobedience. Conventionally, it is Adam's sexuality that occasions sin and Jesus' celibacy that is the remedy. Or it is Adam's pride and disobedience and self-exaltation, his presumption, that occasions sin, and it is Jesus' humility and obedience and self-sacrifice that heals. I regard the interpretation here (Adam excessively and exclusively all-father, Jesus as virginally and exclusively son) not so much a contradiction of such conventional wisdom and formulas as a variation that makes them more plausible.

Consider, first, sin as presumption and trespass. Adam disobediently crossed the boundaries set for him, ate forbidden fruit, aspired to be what he was not. What better way to characterize the son's presumptuous distortion, his impatient unwillingness to accept sonship and his pretense to be father? The trespass is redeemed by the Son's patient willingness to accept sonship, to discount any claims at equality with Father.

Second, the sin of sexuality may be misunderstood if interpreted as simply lust and sensuality. Perhaps what is sinful is an unauthentic and irresponsible claim to fatherhood. Adam and Eve as teenage sex partners: unauthentic because premature, that is, without period of self-conscious sonship, apprenticeship for manhood. Are fathers who are not fathers—absent fathers, abusive fathers, fearful fathers—guilty (and probably victim) of such unwarranted, unapprenticed, un-sonned claims to fatherhood? (Sexuality and pride become the same sin.) The healing power of celibacy may have little to do with puritanical denial of fleshly experience and everything to do with the acceptance of a sonship status, precisely the self-affirmation every son is invited to make, and often doesn't.

"Little Man" or "Real Boy"

"My little man," dotes a mother, naming precisely the temptation and dilemma every boy struggles with: Do I try to be a man like my father? If so, I'm headed for competition, failure, inadequacy, a sense of being a fraud, imposter, loser; for now I can be only a second-rate man. Or am I something different and equally valid, a boy, a son? The choice is between "little man" and "real boy."[4] Can I be son proudly, or must I feel resigned to being "only" the son? It is a struggle likely to echo throughout his manhood. Here we try to track some of its early contours.

Maybe the question —Am I little man or real boy?— comes to critical focus around age five, as Freud supposed, in the form of the romantic triangle of mother-father-son, the perplexity Freud named after Oedipus. The boy sees himself especially and intimately favored by his mother. But he also sees that there is another favored intimacy denied to him and reserved for his father. This relegates him to his own place. Is that place different or inferior? That is the crucial question. Am I second best, a loser, or am I authentic in my own way, a different kind of winner? Does the boy need to capture intimacy with his mother by supplanting his father; or does he value his own peculiar sonly intimacy with his mother and a sonly alliance with his father?

Whether it is this rivalry over mother or other rivalries, other reminders of differences in power and privilege, the dilemma for the boy is the same: Does he abort his sonship for an invented fatherhood that leaves him fatherless (and hence no longer even a son), or does he affirm his sonship and also the father that makes him son? The son who claims, even in his imagination, to supplant his father fears becoming unmanned, according to Freud. The peril entails far more than the threat of castration. It is this: If he forsakes his own sonship and supplants sonhood with counterfeit fatherhood, then neither au-

---

4. The parallel with every girl's experience is striking and instructive. The girl, too, in her own way, must struggle (often also throughout her life) with the same dilemma: If I am different from my father, does that make me a second-rate man or a first-rate something else, something different and equally valid? Whatever "penis envy" may or may not mean, it must apply equally to boys and girls.

thentic father nor authentic son remains, no form of authentic masculinity.

If the boy is lucky, he doesn't have to make this decision alone and he does not make it with ambiguity: He is not the father; he *is* the son, and that is good. If he is lucky, his father sets limits firmly, even fiercely; he will not tolerate trespass, pretensions to be the wife's favorite man or the boss or the hero of the family. If he is unlucky, his father abdicates, withdraws, wimps out, and leaves room for the boy to play, at least in his head, with temptations of taking over, aspiring to a father status that can, at best, trigger gnawing feelings of fraudulence and, at worst, the terror of discovery and retribution.

If he is lucky, his mother sets limits and makes clear that, though there is an intense and intimate mother-son affection, as a sexual partner and to share the special vulnerabilities and confidences and mutual dependencies of marriage, she has long preferred another man. If he is unlucky, she flirts with him, cajoling him with a dependence that becomes a profoundly mixed and discomforting message.

If he is lucky, he is solidly affirmed and supported in living in the special qualities and status of being a son, a comer not yet arrived, a subordinated male honored as such, so that he lives as son content and proud. If he is unlucky, he is teased out of sonship and coached and coaxed into adventuring over his head into fraudulent claims to fatherhood.

The pressures to adultomorphize boyhood, to deny sonship, are formidable. We see them in the culture as a whole, in mothers, in fathers, and in the boys themselves, struggling to grow.

In the Culture

Patriarchy is enemy to sonhood as resoundingly as to womanhood. Sonship is a victim of cultural bias that favors fatherhood and exalts manhood (or at least the prevailing stereotype of fatherhood and manhood) fully as much as is femininity a victim, and perhaps with even more devastating damage to actual manhood and to the culture that so idolizes it. Sons are celebrated and honored, in the media, just for those moments when they abandon sonship and act like men, when the little boy summons help on 911 for his stricken mother, when a teenager stands up to an abusive stepfather or makes jump shots like a pro. What we mean by patriarchy is at least as damaging for its denial and sabotage of sonship values as for its denial and sabotage of feminine values. As men and women, after all the necessary remedies are made in stereotyping and fairness, must still finally celebrate their differences, so too with fathers and sons: Their relationship depends on being very clear about the differences. As with men and women, the differences do not properly imply a hierarchy, a superiority or control by one over the other, a desire for one to *be* the other, just differences.

No small part of the dilemma is the general cultural preference for bigness, big men over shorter men, occidentals over orientals, men over women, and men over boys. It is a tremendously formidable hurdle to get past the bias conferred by physical size and prowess and by the habits of mind spawned by size; bigger just automatically seems better.

In Mothers

"My little man," mothers dote, out of their own (quite genuine and understandable) needs. But being a little man is exactly the problem for the boy (and for his mother too, whose real needs are *not* met in this way). The boy's confusion as to whether he is son or father, boy or man, child or surrogate spouse is already present in his own musings and yearnings; that confusion needs to be abated, not abetted, by his parents. To be cast as his mother's little man keeps him from a full-fledged term as a boy, which is the only sure avenue to becoming a man; boyhood denied becomes manhood denied. Worse, it may consign him to a lifetime of playing little man, pretend man, would-be man. The boy who is required or permitted to play little man may never shake the habit of thinking of himself as just that.

In Fathers

Fathers who are uncomfortably phobic with sonship, because they were denied their own term of sonship, insist "I'll make a man out of him" and try to make good on their threat, whether by impatient battering or too-patient coaching. Or, uncomfortable with fatherhood, they quietly retreat from the role, by withdrawing from the scene (into work, for example), or by becoming "buddies" with their sons, or by playing needy and helpless, creating a vacuum that sucks their sons into playing father. Thus boys are seduced not only into husbanding their mothers but also into parenting their fathers. "The boy is father to the man" takes on a new insidious meaning and demand. In any case, such tactics never make a man out of the boy, only a pretend man, who knows too well, deep where it counts, that he is only a pretender and who may never think otherwise about himself. Real men are not made by denying the sonship to which they are born but by exploring it during its own time and by admitting sonship as a lifelong component of their masculine heritage.

Internal Conflicts

Sons have their own internal impulse to accelerate their evolution into manhood and fatherhood. Even without the collusion of parents who need to exploit the boy for something other than his sonship, sonship is difficult to sustain. Sonship is, by definition, ambiguous and unstable. This is the virtue and strength of the son; he is in transition, in growth, inventing strategies to transform himself and to move beyond present boundaries, to become what he is not. That which he is most obviously *not* is also that which he is most obviously becoming: a father. So that is what he most naturally aspires to be.

To aspire to become what he is not: That is the defining energy of the son. It is also the formula for the ultimate destructive existential disaster we know by many names—pride, sin, trespass, alienation. It defines how Oedipus and Adam acted out the same fate. Each has committed himself to the impossible burden of living his life as perpetual pretender, sacrificing a valid sonship for fraudulent fatherhood. He who becomes what he is not is afflicted with knowing that he is not what he has become.

The horror of Oedipus is not, finally, in the deeds of patricide and incest but in the horror that underlies these horrors. The impact of these deeds is resolvable. But what is not resolvable, because it reaches to the core of identity, is the appalling incomprehensible comprehension that the man has become what he is not. He has overreached into free fall. *That,* actual patricide and actual incest or not, is the horrified Oedipus in every man, as Freud tried to find a formula to express. He has allowed himself to see himself as what he is not: That is why the penalty must be not the plucking of a tongue or the severing of a limb or even a castration, but a blinding.

In the case of Adam, the sin is not simply in the eating or in sexuality or even in the disobedience, but in Adam's daring to transform himself—claiming to be what he is not—from son and citizen of the garden to its master, becoming a father on his own timetable, not God's. The penalty for such displacement has to be displacement.

With stakes so high, it is no wonder that a boy shrinks from a course so delicately negotiated—the discovery of his own authentic manhood—and settles for easy modeling and imitation of his own father. Impersonation is safer than free-lance pretense.

Five Sons

Alan

Alan wants to father his father. This means, in the conventional sense of "father," that Alan wants to control him, manage him. Alan wants to prevent his father from making foolish decisions, taking rash action, like ripping out the landscaping; where there is disagreement, he wants his father to honor Alan's authority and abide by his decisions. Alan wants to train his father to be responsible or to yield responsibility to him. Alan aspires to these conventional "fatherly" postures.

But father means more than that. It also means tender nurture and caring, and Alan wants to father his father by providing these things too. He feels responsible, as a father does, to sponsor an affectionate relationship between them. When it fails, Alan feels it a personal failure. The encounter over the landscaping is as much an attempt to pursue this relationship as it is anything else (albeit a rather clumsy attempt, not unlike strategies his father must have once tried with Alan). The main thing Alan feels is responsible, and this is a very familiar feeling. He has carried this feeling in the presence of his father for his whole life, it seems.

But this fatherly impetus is matched by a sonly impetus, which is present but unacknowledged, a closeted resource. What I want to say to Alan is not, Change your ways, but, Notice your ways and honor them; enjoy yourself as the son you are. This pertains literally: Be son to your father; let him keep responsibility for his own life, even for rash decisions; you don't have to be what you're not, the one in control. Even go off and play for the weekend, as sons can do.

It also pertains more profoundly: If you feel baffled and helpless about your relationship with your father (as well as about his landscaping plans), that is perfectly appropriate for the son you are. Don't deny the perplexity, or even the fear. You *are* still a son facing fresh "identity crises" whose resolution lies ahead, out of sight. It has happened before, with your father and with others, and it will again: Just in the times you have let go of the anxious pretense that you are required to make things come out right, opportunities and resolutions have appeared. Not always, but it happens.

When he is willing to be son, baffled, expectant, not in control, Alan may come closer to what he most urgently wants, finding the old man restored to him as a father. The destiny may be accomplished not by coercing it but by living in its shadows.

Carl

To Carl the message may sound, at first, just like what he hears from Donna, but it may actually be the opposite. Both Donna and I may be saying, Go easy on the puppies and ice-cream cones; don't push them. For Donna, this seems to mean, You're too much like a whimsical son, and I am looking for a responsible father. She even says sometimes, "You're just another kid around the house for me to worry about." But here we say, Don't push the puppy and the cones because the pushing is untrue to the sonly impetus that prompts them. Making weapons or issues out of them is to convert the sonly vitality that inspired the puppy and the cones into a kind of premature fatherhood. It is to foreclose *further* workings of the whimsy and imagination and experimentation. It is to abort expectancy. A puppy is probably not the final answer, only the first fruits of boyish imagination. A puppy, to borrow language from an earlier chapter, is more like the star than the new king, and it takes the boyish wonder of the magi to wait and see where it is leading. What destiny actually holds for this family is probably "post-puppy"—maybe an outing to the zoo for Carl and the kids, maybe an overnight getaway for Carl and Donna, maybe a less frisky pet, like a turtle. All it may take to find out is a genuinely boyish "OK, where do we go from here?"

Howard

The checkout clerk is insulting only if Howard is locked into being regarded exclusively as the super-responsible, super-competent adult that he is. Instead, it may be taken as a golden invitation to become again the playful son that he also is. "Boy," he hears himself called, and he chooses to suppose that she is dismissing him for his age (as in another setting another man might suppose "boy" is dismissing him for his race). Such supposing may be correct—it probably is. But that is what it means to *her*, not what it needs to mean to *him*.

As a man, Howard feels responsible for what she is feeling; as a son, he is entitled to his own feelings. Adult men are expected to maintain an alert surveillance of their surroundings, to take everything into account, to make everything right. That's what it means to be the responsible manager that a man is expected to be. If something is amiss, it is his job to fix it. So Howard fumes. He feels somehow responsible for what she thinks and is challenged by it. But boys are not burdened with such all-inclusive responsibility (though adults often want to rush their initiation into it), and in this case Howard need not be either. Boys can pick and choose what they want to take seriously and what they choose to smirk at. The boy in Howard, if unlocked, wants to give her the finger and let it go at that. Let it go at that, and get on with agendas of his own choosing, freed from the script of being governed by her script.

What's so bad about the idea of aging as a second childhood? Only that people don't think of you as a major player, a master of the universe. But what's so bad about that, after all? The boy who calls out "The emperor has no clothes!" releases the emperor from crippling pretense. Let the boy in Howard sing out a similar liberation of the would-be emperor in himself. If grocery checkouts and automobile check-ins provoke the cry, they become a blessing.

There is a boyish playfulness in Howard's counting out his coins to get back quarters. It's a game he enjoys. Except that for now the boyish play has been distorted into adultlike work, involving the issues of status and performance and competence that inevitably accompany adult work. Let the play be play, and shred those scripts. Let the boy be a boy. Howard will find himself responding to the clerk with amiable quips like, "Oh, let me have my fun," and she may even play too. Let the aging be an aging, a maturing into boyhood.

Murray

For the son the grandeur is in the other, in the person of the father, and in a not-nowness in the form of the future. For the one-sided father, the grandeur is lodged in the self and in the imperative of the immediate, the now. It's up to me, here and now: That's the overweening pretense—and the daunting burden—when the man comes to think about himself not just as father but as Father. Like Adam and Oedipus, he has allowed himself to pretend to be what he is not. It is an expectation of the self doomed to fail and an unsustainable claim to have mastered the moment. Murray is confronting that pretension. For Murray the pain in his addiction to work is that it does not work for him. It does not yield the sense of abundance that he thinks it promises and that he expects. The pain is in the reminder that the grandeur and authority is in another, not in himself. The unwelcome but saving message Murray gets from his work is that he cannot conquer it. He finds painful the reminder of this (religious) message of sonship. But the power is in the sorrow, not in its denial. His destiny is in this shadow, not in extinguishing it. Murray need not be heckled into changing his ways, neither his habits of work nor the sorrow it brings. He need only be encouraged to enlarge his sense of himself by accepting the reminder the work and sorrow offer: You are not merely the father, you are also a son who willingly and expectantly knows the grandeur beyond your own doings and capacities. (This is an affirmation allied, if you will, with the Son of God, who disclosed saving in just such yielding.) As a good son might be lovingly amused at the preposterous curmudgeon who is his father, let Murray be lovingly amused at this in himself.

Norman

Norman's interpretation of sex as a transformation from dailiness to transcendence is persuasive and important. It might be more persuasive, more amenable to Pat, and open up a richer sexual life for Norm, if there were less reliance on consummation and more appreciation of tease and foreplay. That is the issue between Pat and Norm, and that is the issue where Norm's life could be enlarged by more appreciation of his own sonliness. Tease and foreplay are in the mode of sonship, the mode of expectancy, and, as such, are authentic and pleasurable in themselves, not just as promises of consummation. Just as it is a loss for a man to find sonship unpleasant because it is not fatherhood, it is a loss for the man to find sex play unpleasant because it is not consummation. Indeed, when men (not just women) find sex disappointing (*Is that all there is?*), it is usually for a dearth of play and teasing. Just as a man can come to savor the masculinity that is in him as a son, so can Norman come to savor the sexuality that is in the expectancy.

Both Pat and Norm can come to appreciate the "conversation" not as an alternative to sex but as a form of sex. Can't they remember flirting, the art of loading everyday conversation and gestures with sexual innuendo? It's delicious, even when it doesn't come close to consummation—and when it does. Pat can drink her tea with a saucy suggestiveness, her eyes over the cup on Norm's reactions. Norm can include among his tales of the day a story of going off into sexual daydreams ("there you were stark naked standing right behind old Barker's chair, and he wouldn't have known what to do with you if he had seen you") and maybe some harmless gossip about an office romance ("Can you imagine the two of them alone?" . . . "Maybe they can't imagine us in bed together" . . . "*I* can!"). Norm can respond to Pat's recital of the minor defeats of the day with mock knightly pantomime ("*I'll* pay the rent!"). As for the back rubbing, why not pretend, for a time, to be adolescents making out and committed to not going all the way? That was a heady experience once and still can be, for the boy in Norm.

To live as a son is to live not in sure capture of sure goal but in expectancy, open-ended, on the way to a goal yet to be discerned, still shadowy yet still trusted in faith, hope, and love: So it is, too, with sex. When Norm speaks of sex as "transporting," he speaks well, especially as he stays open to surprise about the destination and therefore open to the delight of the transport itself. The enemy of sonship, as it is the enemy of sex, is routine, a settledness (like the monarch or the colonist) that robs expectancy, and robs destiny too, by settling for one of its shadows.

There is a good chance that what Pat and Norm most dread is that the other's strategy threatens to lapse into such routine. Norm fears that back rub and bedtime conversation threaten to become routine, ends in themselves; Pat dreads the same about intercourse. In sharing that dread, they share, with sons everywhere, their trust and delight in discovery.

A Personal Last Word

10

"Men are expectant. Men live a life that feels chronically destined, ever on the verge—intended for something that is never quite arrived at, an unending not-yet, the perpetual pilgrimage of almost, a prolonged tumescence. . . . A man learns how to live in the shadow of his own destiny."

So opened this book, portraying it as discontent and sorrow that a man lives on the verge, enduring a prolonged tumescence of the soul.

So ends the book, final chapter echoing the first, now redeemed, portraying it as a matter of zest and delight that a man lives his life on the verge, tumescent, masculinity at its fullest. A man does learn that in the shadow of his own destiny is a choice place to live out his life.

Living chronically destined *is* painful for those who need to foreclose on life and make destination all—for the monarch, the crusader, the colonist, the patriarch. Tumescence *is* painful for those intent only on scoring. Expectancy becomes the measure of the limits of a man's life by reminding him what his life is not.

But living destined, expectant, on the verge—for those who can behold it—opens life to an enlargement and a virility. Tumescence begets its own delight. Expectancy will assure the expanse of a man's life, not just measure its limits. The shadows of destiny are richer in contour than the burnished luster of destination achieved. The shadows of destiny are richer in contour than the bleak emptiness of destination denied.

A Personal Last Word

The contours of the shadows are visible to those who expect light at the end of the tunnel but whose eyes are, for now, adapted to the dark.

So this book would keep its promise, not to scold men for being as they are, not to coach them to change, not to bash. Instead, it invites, Be as you are and esteem it, as intended. Esteem it, if you will, as living the life that God intends, and the life that God joins, in the enterprise of ever creating, ever redeeming. Count it as warning if contentment is savored overlong; something is being missed. Count it as warning if despair is savored overmuch; something is being missed.

Is that all there is? Treasure the question, for without it the ringing affirmation *There must be more!* is muted.

The priest, knowing the sacramental stuff he manipulates is but surrogate for the transcendent, keeps looking and pointing beyond that stuff to the transcendent it hints at. The magi keep following their star *beyond* the king's palace in search of the new king. The pilgrim, intent on reaching the shrine, knows too that to make its blessing *his* he must leave the shrine again and resume his journey, most often toward the perplexities back home. The son knows that the expectancies that thrill him must remain, for now, beyond his grasp or they lose their power.

Yet the pain in *Is that all there is?* always threatens to snuff out the hope. So the pain never loses its power to lure a man to foreclose the question and to settle with a premature *This is it.* The priest comes to credit the sacraments he can grasp as though they *were* the transcendent that eludes his grasp. The magi enlist in the service of the "real" king, the one with the robes and palace and army. The pilgrim settles at the shrine and would control its power, perhaps as conqueror or colonist. The son snatches at what he can of manhood and pretends it is.

Is that all there is? is the right question for both writer and reader to pose at the end of a book, conceding the disappointments and savoring the hope that, here and there, the words may have meant more than they said. Ideas like "chronically destined" or "living conscripted" and images like magi and pilgrim and son say something to me and about me. The stories of Alan, Carl, Howard, Murray, and Norm are somehow my stories. And perhaps for you too, if you have come this far. But they fall short, too, and must finally be important because they

141

point beyond themselves and suggest more than they can say. I genuinely hope there has been time with the book face down while you pondered and puzzled. I know I have spent far more time with hands *off* the keyboard and eyes staring at something beyond the screen. Far more words have been discarded than saved, and surely you would prune some more. In the long run, *all* these words must be discarded and replaced—Magi and Pilgrim, Carl and Norm—for the sake of saying more truly what they have tried to say here. Most of all, writer and reader should jettison just those phrases and images that have prompted a hearty *That's it!* lest their message be lost for failing to ask *Is that all there is?*

If I try, one last time, to find words to say what I think most needs to be said, it goes like this.

Authenticity for men—feeling "saved" (in language that once meant more than it usually does now)—is to be found within those modes of living that appear most characteristic of men, not in being shamed or coached out of those modes.

The modes of masculinity that hold the most hope are often painful and difficult, the modes of faith and hope and love, modes that are painful because they require waiting and disappointment and perplexity, and renunciation of settled ways for the unsettled. Yet authenticity, nobility, "saving" *is* found in affirming these modes, not denying them.

They are the modes of religion at its best—the modes, we may even dare to say, of God himself.